AMERICAN
MUSICAL REVUE

AMERICAN MUSICAL REVUE

From *The Passing Show* to *Sugar Babies*

GERALD BORDMAN

New York   Oxford
OXFORD UNIVERSITY PRESS
1985

Oxford University Press

Oxford   London   New York   Toronto
Delhi   Bombay   Calcutta   Madras   Karachi
Kuala Lumpur   Singapore   Hong Kong   Tokyo
Nairobi   Dar es Salaam   Cape Town
Melbourne   Auckland

and associated companies in
Beirut   Berlin   Ibadan   Mexico City   Nicosia

Published by Oxford University Press, Inc.,
200 Madison Avenue, New York, New York 10016

Library of Congress Cataloging in Publication Data
Bordman, Gerald Martin.
American musical revue.
Includes index.
1. Musical revue, comedy, etc.—United States.
I. Title.
ML1711.B665   1985   782.81'0973   85–4816
ISBN 0–19–503630–1

Printing (last digit): 9 8 7 6 5 4 3 2 1

Printed in the United States of America

Preface

Vaudeville—the great vaudeville of big-time two-a-day and the Palace—has been only a memory for more than half a century. Yet it is still looked back on with passion and affection, still the subject of lively reminiscences and occasional books. To some oldtimers and aficionados it seems very much alive, if only in the mind's eye.

Not so its wonderful cousin, the revue. Although off-Broadway continues to mount small-scale revues, it does so fitfully, and rarely with pronounced élan or success. Broadway hasn't seen a real, honest-to-goodness revue in years, and doesn't seem to care if it ever will again. The tiniest band of devoted sentimentalists appear to be its only mourners. Several decades have passed since a new book appeared to record and study this once vital, ebullient genre.

Of course, vaudeville was always more popular than the revue. Statistics show that vaudeville for many years was overwhelmingly the most generally accepted form of entertainment in America. Broadway revues were more elitist, as was Broadway itself. But the olios that were brought together as Broadway revues had their own strengths and glories, and the revue flourished long after vaudeville became, at best, a tab show alongside films. This book attempts a brief look at what made revues develop, what made them tick, and, eventually, what caused them to die away. In so doing, it concludes a trilogy of studies which looked first at operetta, then at musical comedy.

I am grateful for the help given me by the staffs of the Library of Congress, the Library of the Performing Arts (New York City), the Theatre Collection at the Museum of the City of New York, the Theatre Collection of the Free Library of Philadelphia, and the library at Millersville (Pa.) University.

Last, but assuredly not least, my thanks goes out to my editor's always helpful secretary and my typist, Joellyn Ausanka, and, most of all, to my unflappable editor, Sheldon Meyer.

Yellow Woods Farms   Gerald Bordman
Kirk's Mills, Pa.
February 1985

Contents

AMERICAN
MUSICAL REVUE

1

Tentative Beginnings

There are two sides to every argument, and any discussion of the differing points of view of the history of American musical revue establishes that it is no exception to the rule. On the one hand, strict constructionists could argue that this delightful, once so popular genre lasted just over half a century—that it reached America in the mid-1890s and by the 1950s was all but finished. In a sense this narrow view is quite correct. On the other hand, it has been argued, precursors have been found in virtually the earliest decades of our theatre, and the musical revue—in a form markedly different from that of its heyday—remains alive, if not exactly well, down to the present. Perhaps such a point of view can be accepted only if we agree to stretch a few points, but this approach does allow for an intriguing thesis—namely, that the classic revue came to rely increasingly on its songs and thus fell victim to the decline of American theatre music more quickly and more totally than did the other musical theatre genres, operetta and musical comedy. As if to set a seal on this approach, most of the successful revues of recent years—*Ain't Misbehavin'*, *Eubie*, and

Sophisticated Ladies—have been nothing but retrospective concerts of older music.

Ask any playgoer over the age of fifty—any playgoer lucky enough to have enjoyed some of the last traditional revues, to characterize them—and he or she would almost certainly describe them as simply a random collection of songs and comic sketches, almost entirely unrelated to one another. The description would be right on the button. But in the mid-1980s there are still a few genuine oldtimers alive who saw and remember an earlier generation of revues, and these oldsters, if their memories are accurate, might be reluctant to accept so simple a description. They would remember a time, largely before World War I, but continuing with diminishing vigor into the 1920s and occasionally beyond, when other elements constituted an expected part of any revue. They would undoubtedly talk first of the lavish spectacle—of magnificent, sumptuous scenery, of exquisitely composed tableaux, and of long lines of beautiful girls parading in sometimes gorgeous, sometimes grotesque costumes. If their memories are deep and retentive enough they might even recall that revues were tied together first by plots and later, occasionally, by themes. Even the wispiest of plots or the simplest of themes implies a certain overall conceptualization, a necessity to toy with ideas and images beyond anything most music can induce, so that in the earliest revues there was created a tension between the fundamentally emotional effects of music on one side and the words or thoughts on the other. (Of course a song's lyric sets up this tug as well, but the tension is different.) The earliest spectacles, in a way, also trafficked with this type of conceptualization, since they were not merely the exotic, often explicitly sensual tableaux of Ziegfeldian extravaganza. Instead they were often allegorical pictures, usually flagwaving on a national or regional level and demanding first an intellectual response and only afterwards an emotional reaction.

A certain intellectuality (everything is relative on the American musical stage) was never lost. Skits and song lyrics from many a great revue were not only knowing and biting but required knowledgeability on the part of playgoers—an awareness of current events and personalities, of trends in all the arts. In themselves these skits and lyrics frequently gave a momentary but valid theatrical tension to the shows. Yet that any overall conceptualization was not critical to the revue can be strenuously argued from the fact that plots and, with occasional exceptions, themes, disappeared from revues at precisely the time the genre entered its glory days. If aging playgoers still speak in awed tones of the beauties with which Ziegfeld endowed his productions, they are responding to an unforgettable theatrical immediacy. As we will see, Ziegfeld's greatest contribution was not so obvious. He was the first producer to bring to the revue one of the two requisites for its greatness—a sense of balance. Before his time revues had offered fine comedy and comics (his were often superior), good dancing (Ziegfeld here did not notably improve matters), attractive sets and costumes (his reached new heights), and pleasant music. Pleasant music—but how many revue songs before the *Follies* come to mind? Ziegfeld was the man who, despite his much bruited indifference to songs, inserted the first long-lived "standards" to come from the revue stage. When "Shine On, Harvest Moon" was sung in the *Follies of 1908*, fine and enduring songs began to alternate with splendid comedy, and with these songs the revue was to achieve a sense of balance that marked it throughout its heyday. So a principal thesis of this book is not that the loss of great songs in themselves signified the end of the genre's best years but rather that the omission of fine songs disturbed the basic sense of balance and thus irreparably damaged the genre.

The second requisite is perhaps less subtle: a sense of purpose—entertainment. From the start, entertainment was on the minds of producers and writers, and of the tired businessman who bought tickets. It remained a goal through thick and thin at least until the 1930s, when cries for meaningfulness and social significance became the rationale for propagandizing that alienated probably as many playgoers as it satisfied. After the mid-1940s, when it was perceived that book musicals, with their opportunities for plot and character development, could dig deeper into social and human problems and thus further the cause of meaningfulness and social significance, the image of the revue was further tarnished in many eyes. (There were, of course, other reasons for the growth of the book musical which will be discussed later.) So by the late 1950s and especially during the turmoil of the 1960s, the malaise of rebellion that spread across the country and inevitably touched Broadway sent the revue into a tailspin from which it has never recovered. But that is modern history. Long ago matters were different.

Hints of happy things to come began very early on. Musical theatre itself, of which the revue was to be a salient branch for a time, first charmed American audiences as early as 1735. These eighteenth-century musicals were, of course, ballad operas and are better looked upon as precursors of musical comedy or even operetta, since they were more completely plotted than revues and integrated song and story more carefully than revues ever were to do. By Revolutionary times and to a still greater extent once the new nation was independent, ballad operas sometimes made way for lavishly bedecked "oratorical" entertainments such as Francis Hopkinson's *The Temple of Minerva*, which the French minister offered in Washington's honor at Philadelphia in 1781 and which depicted the Goddess Minerva and her High Priest joining together the Geniuses of France and America. Clearly a descendant of the masques of a previous century, these musical spectacles served as important propaganda pieces and morale boosters for a nation still insecure.

In the 1820s an Englishman and an English play gave further hints of things to come. The Englishman was Charles Mathews, who made two trips to America, the first in 1822, when he was at the height of his droll powers, the last in 1834, when he was terminally ill. Although he appeared in a number of traditional comic roles, such as Sir Peter Teazle in *The School for Scandal* and Sir Fretful Plagiary in *The Critic*, he was most welcomed for what were essentially one-man entertainments he offered under titles on the order of *Mathews at Home* and *The Comic Annual*. In these he mimicked famous figures of the time and presented a wide-ranging assortment of oddball characters, such as Josephus Jollyfat, a Gastronomer Astronomer. He larded these skits "with Welsh, French, Scotch, Irish, Indian, Swiss and English airs." One can only wonder how very different this was than, say, *An Evening with Beatrice Lillie* or *At Home with Ethel Waters* a hundred or so years later, although both modern-day stars, who had spent much of their careers in traditional revues, undoubtedly leaned far more toward the musical side. Even Mathews's use of the word "annual" in a title, although he most likely used it as a variant of annal, suggests the annual editions of later revues.

The English play was W. T. Moncrieff's theatricalization of Pierce Egan's *Tom and Jerry; or, Life in London*. Reaching New York in 1823, it pioneered a simple, ingenious way of tying together basically unrelated songs and incidents by incorporating them into a tour of a great city. In this instance, the paper-thin plot recounted the adventures of a country bumpkin, Jerry Hawthorn, after he arrives from the provinces to spend some time with his more worldly, citified cousin, Corinthian Tom. Their escapades provided a scene painter's field day, moving the action from one celebrated London setting to the next, while the looseness of the tale allowed for the insertion of all manner of contemporary songs and dances. For years afterwards this device was the sole excuse writers and producers needed to justify similarly roustabout entertainments. To cite one example, the beloved old English-born actor-manager William E. Burton used it on a number of occasions, once transporting his loyal audiences to *The World's Fair; or, London in 1851*, and three years later, in *Apollo in New York*, showing what might happen if a Greek god visited 1854 America. (Nearly sixty years later, in 1910, Olympus emptied out when the gods came for a second look in *Up and Down Broadway*.)

But before Burton became the darling of New York theatregoers, another Englishman held sway for a decade and in his own way broke ground in areas the revue would later develop. The American stage had probably enjoyed few such skilled burlesque artists as the tall, somewhat gaunt William Mitchell. Shortly after his arrival in this country he took over New York's bandbox Olympic Theatre and for eleven years made it often the city's most popular playhouse. Even his posters and programs were fun, making merry as they advertised such romps as his spoof of Fanny Elssler's *La Tarentule*, which he mocked as *La Musquitoe*, her *La Cracovienne*, which he twitted in *Crack-a-Vein*, and *La Bayadère, the Maid of Cashmere*, which he sent up as *Buy-It-Dear, 'Tis Made of Cashmere*. Thus, the hoardings that proclaimed the arrival of Elssler were satirized in his own "TERRIFIC ANNOUNCEMENT!" which continued:

The Public are respectfully informed that

MR. MITCHELL

HAVING ARRIVED FROM EUROPE

Four years ago—has, with very little difficulty, prevailed upon himself to appear on MONDAY next, in a NEW PANTOMIMIC BALLET, entitled

LA MUSQUITOE!

which never was performed at

L'ACADEMIE ROYALE DE MUSIQUE AT PARIS

and it is very probable never will be

PERFORMED THERE 300 SUCCESSIVE NIGHTS!

From take-offs such as this came the kidding of later hits that was to be a stock-in-trade of the great revues, which included such gems as "Rose of Arizona" in *The Garrick Gaieties* and "The Gladiola Girl" in *Lend an Ear*.

Mitchell's heyday was the 1840s, and it was during this period, in 1843 in fact, that a pudgy, rather moon-faced Irishman with a high forehead and conspicuous moustache arrived in New York with hopes of taking the place of Tyrone Power, the recently drowned Irish favorite. The Irishman's name was John Brougham. His success was anything but instant, since for many years no one could replace Power in the public's affection, and his career was to be curiously checkered. Brougham spent several seasons with Burton and later with Wallack's much ad-mired ensemble. Gradually he endeared himself to playgoers in such roles as Captain Cuttle, Dazzle, Micawber, and Sir Lucius O'Trigger. With time he became one of our theatre's most beloved comedians. But he also persistently tried his hand at producing and running theatres, sooner or later always coming a cropper. Lastly he turned to playwriting, and before his death in 1880 he created over one hundred theatre pieces that ranged over a wide variety of genres and styles and met more than his share of failure. Yet some of his works, such as his melodrama *The Duke's Motto*, were hugely successful. However, it was his more off-beat ventures that secured him a place in the history of the American musical revue. For example, his 1851 *A Row at the Lyceum*, purportedly depicting the fracas that ensues when members of the audience react to a performance on stage, was one of the earliest plays to plant stooges in the audience and have them interact with the players on stage to good effect, although Mitchell had also employed the gimmick successfully. Time and again later revues by using this device would achieve a certain ersatz spontaneity and bring themselves in more immediate touch with their audiences than musical comedy or operetta ever could. Brougham's comedy most likely was largely forgotten by the time revues employed the device and the general perception would be that the revue borrowed the trick from vaudeville. Nonetheless Brougham's pioneering cannot be overlooked.

Even more to the point was his rehashing of the Tom and Jerry motif in 1856 with a mélange of songs, dances, and loosely related incidents in *Life in New York; or, Tom and Jerry on a Visit*. Many of his celebrated burlesques, notably his 1855 *Pocahontas*, also displayed traits later common to the musical revue—the mocking of contemporary events and figures, the satirizing of famous plays, the interjection of songs and dances having little or nothing to do with the matter at hand, and the resorting to outlandish anachronisms.

All in all, the most intriguing of Brougham's offerings to students of the revue form has to be *The Dramatic Review for 1868*. This work was first offered at the tiny Fifth Avenue Theatre on January 25, 1869, as an afterpiece to the main attraction, Brougham's new comedy *Better Late Than Never*. That the work was an afterpiece does not detract in the least from its significance, since bills of two and sometimes even three plays, albeit on the wane, were still not uncommon. And while the work was not the full-length entertainment that later revues were, it was rife with characteristics of the classic revues. Indeed, for all practical purposes, it was a revue and as such may have been the first real American one. Even the use of the term "review" in the title is intriguing, for it brings out, more clearly than the French spelling adopted later, a basic quality of virtually all revues—namely, that revues were essentially a tongue-in-cheek, somewhat haphazard examination of contemporary foibles and follies. The lamentable or laughable excesses of contemporary figures, events, works of art, and even artistic styles were all to be grist of the revue mill.

Brougham's revue opened with a touch of extravagant spectacle— another precursor of things to come—in this case an allegorical tableau depicting Manhatta, Brooklyna (who was described as "the oldest of Manhatta's family, and a remarkably forward young lady, proud, pious, and independent, holding but ferry little intercourse with her Ma, and that she means to abridge"), along with New Jersia, North Rivero, East Rivero, Mlle. Fashion, Public Opinion, Melpomene ("an old and melancholy muse, who has seen better days"), and, eventually, Captain Jinks. The allegorical picture quickly deteriorated into a burlesque romp, in which Captain Jinks was portrayed as a trouser role by one of Brougham's favorite performers, Effie Germon. Inevitably, the popular plays of the day came in for a ribbing, including Augustin Daly's *Under the Gaslight*, Dion Boucicault's *After Dark* and Brougham's own play for Mr. and Mrs. Barney Williams, *The Emerald Ring*. Nor was the musical theatre of the time ignored. The ragingly popular opéra bouffes were spoofed in "Bouffe à la Mode," while the contemporary theatre's most beloved entertainer, George L. Fox, and his biggest success, *Humpty Dumpty*, were twitted in "The Fox's Nest." The velocipede fad, then sweeping the country, was duly noted in a song put across by the versatile Miss Germon. But *The Dramatic Review for 1868* is rarely, if ever, discussed in histories of American musical revue. The reason is simple. The show was a short-lived failure, precipitating another of Brougham's many financial crises. If nothing succeeds like success, nothing recedes like failure. Still, Brougham must be awarded some small niche in the American revue pantheon.

Any number of other figures in the legitimate scene of these early years no doubt contributed unwittingly to paving the way for future revues. As a rule they were most often figures popular on burlesque stages—James Robinson Planché and his musical pieces, Mrs. John Wood. But the seeds of revue were also being sown, and in an equally, possibly more significant fashion elsewhere: in the olios and the later satiric skits of minstrelsy, in minstrel music, in the olios of the medicine shows or those offered between the acts on show boats, and, most of all, during the years after the Civil War, in the fast rising field of vaudeville or, as it was then called, variety.

An argument could be made that, indeed, minstrel shows, allowing for their unique specializations, were the earliest American musical revues. After all, they were plotless musical entertainments filled with skits, with a wide variety of songs, and with performers displaying their distinctive skills. Moreover, the performers appeared throughout the show, taking part often both in jokes and skits on one hand, musical numbers on the other. This was especially true of later, more elaborate minstrel shows, which frequently added an element of spectacle to boot. By contrast, a performer in vaudeville usually appeared only once during the evening, offering merely the particular turn for which he or she was best known, albeit many early variety players had to double in brass.

Medicine show and show boat olios were more primitive, slap-dash affairs, perhaps best described as country bumpkins' vaudeville. But vaudeville itself must clearly be accounted a forerunner of revue, and for several decades the two genres flourished side by side. Time and again variety stages served as spawning grounds for future revue stars, and, of course, revue stars often returned to vaudeville as headliners. Song and dance dominated variety from its sometimes seedy start, but by the 1870s and 1880s leading vaudeville impresarios such as Tony Pastor were offering skits and abbreviated musicals as part of their bills. There were, too, any number of successful monologuists and comedy teams.

The relative importance of musical numbers and performers in minstrelsy and vaudeville makes it seem all the odder that early revues were so indifferent to obtaining better songs. Variety and especially minstrelsy left behind numerous still popular songs. One reason may be that revue appeared during an interregnum. The great mid-nineteenth-century popular writers such as Stephen Foster, George F. Root, Will S. Hays, and Henry Clay Work were gone or written out, and no one of similar caliber had yet emerged to take their place. Moreover, songwriters possibly still saw the minstrel stage and vaudeville as better and more profitable platforms for their output. However, it must also be kept in mind that, while minstrelsy and vaudeville may have been important in aiding the rise of the revue, the revue remained a "legit" entertainment and that its legitimate antecedents did anything but emphasize the musical side. Mathews and Burton, even Mitchell and Brougham, would no doubt be surprised to learn of the revue as a genre and to realize that they might possibly be viewed as trailblazers. Mathews, Burton, and Brougham dealt basically in the traditional theatrical forms of their eras, comedy and drama. They had recourse to musical numbers in their plays because throughout the nineteenth century all first class and many lesser playhouses maintained orchestras for overtures, entr'actes, and incidental music, and because the interjection of an occasional song was almost expected by their audiences, much as Shakespeare had sprinkled his comedies and sometimes his tragedies with song, and much as, many years later in the 1930s and 1940s, dramatic films sometimes included a song or two without altering the perception that they were straight films. The intent of all these men, with the questionable exception of Mitchell, was to bring to theatrical life fundamentally literary material, trafficking most immediately in words and ideas. Almost certainly they considered the music or songs they employed as decoration or, at best, elaboration. Thus, in a major sense, in the genesis of the revue words came before music.

Revue, as mentioned earlier, is an English appropriation of a French word, so we ought to look briefly at Parisian influences on early American revue. A brief look, too, is all that these influences merit, since their effect on the nineteenth-century American musical stage was slight and at second hand. Even the French spelling was a later, slightly pretentious borrowing. Although French plays, French opéra bouffe, and a few French performers enjoyed great American popularity, the often satiric hodgepodges mounted by some Parisian cabarets and at such theatres as the Folies-Marigny, the Bouffe-Parisiens, and Variétés were too localized in subject to cross the Channel, let alone the Atlantic. Yet the proximity of London to Paris made English writers and performers very aware of these productions and did prompt certain imitation. It may be noteworthy that all the American figures who had a hand in prototypical revues were English-born, or, in the case of the

Irish Brougham, London-trained. Many English theatrical historians credit Planché with bringing the form to London, and he himself noted in his reminiscences, "My theatrical labours in the year 1825 terminated with the production . . . of a one-act piece on the 12 December, entitled *Success! or, a Hit, if You Like It*, which I only mention because it was the first attempt in this country to introduce that class of entertainment so popular in Paris called *Revue.*" Planché, whose memoirs were published in 1872, called these works *"pièces de circonstance"* and recognized they were "inevitably ephemeral from their nature." Indeed, they were so ephemeral that, while many of his other works enjoyed marked American success, these were never imported.

In 1880 the distinguished American critic, Brander Matthews, wrote in his *The Theatre of Paris,*

> [The] minor Parisian theatres have one peculiarity. On or about the first of January they often produce a piece chronicling and satirising the events of the past year, and obviously called a "review" (*revue*) of the year. Mr. John Brougham endeavoured to naturalize the review in New York when he opened his pretty little Fifth Avenue Theatre in 1869, but the attempt failed. . . . The opportunity the review offers for "local hits" and personalities is too tempting to be missed; but . . . the practice of preparing a New Year's annual in Paris began slowly to die out about a decade ago. Within the past two or three years the fashion seems to be coming a little more in favor again.

Still, it was another fourteen years before the revue finally took hold in America.

2

The Passing Show: *The Gay Nineties and the Turn-of-the-Century*

Important turns of events often have a way of being guessed at in advance. If little ballyhoo attended the opening of *The Dramatic Review for 1868*, this was only partially because newspapers of that day did not devote quite so much space to theatre as they were to do a few years later. The premiere of *The Passing Show* was a different matter. By 1894 papers were giving more space to plays, so experienced drama editors clearly sensed that something of historical if not artistic significance was in the air. Yet their awareness that the arrival of this new musical was somehow meaningful did not carry with it a total understanding or agreement about that meaning.

For one, as they often still do today, most New York newspapers seemed to have little real sense of past history. There was scarcely any attempt to suggest that, the new musical, however innovative it might be, did not spring whole out of nowhere, but had a long, if tentative, development. The *Times* was one of the few exceptions, telling its readers that the musical was "a kind of entertainment little known in this country, and not attempted since John Brougham's time." That was not much of a history lesson, but more than most other newspapers offered.

Their emphasis seemed to be on the immediate "news" and the seeming newness of the type of entertainment about to be unveiled. The *World* went into some detail, spotlighting the revival of revue in Paris that Matthews had alluded to fourteen years before and, almost alone among its competitors, employing the French spelling. It would be years before most other newspapers, or even theatrical advertisements, for that matter, accepted the French orthography.

Part of the problem was that the producers of the new show were themselves wary of calling their musical a revue or a review, though the latter term took hold rather quickly. In many advertisements they branded their show, somewhat cautiously, "a topical extravaganza," a phrase seemingly designed to reassure potential playgoers who might have been puzzled or dissuaded by the use of the newer and unfamiliar expression. It pandered to the widespread, comfortable popularity of a term linked in playgoers' minds with mammoth mountings like the still popular *The Black Crook* while at the same time it made reference to the rage for "topical songs," ditties satirizing current events, that were then being inserted even into comic operas set in the long ago and far away.

The Passing Show opened at the Casino Theatre on May 12, 1894. Its producer was George Lederer, who, for a few short years at the turn of the century, before the advent of Joe Weber, Lew Fields, and Florenz Ziegfeld, was Broadway's leading purveyor of lighter but lavish musicals. If his musicals were not as gargantuan as those mounted regularly at Niblo's and the newer huge auditoriums, they were opulent enough so that his employment of the word "extravaganza" was not totally out of line. The author of the text was Sydney Rosenfeld, a competent craftsman and a notorious gadfly; the composer, Ludwig Englander, an Austrian immigrant who was just beginning a long, prolific, and thoroughly undistinguished career as a writer of theatre music. Heading the cast of a hundred were a popular comedian, Jefferson De Angelis, and a fleetingly celebrated comedienne, Adele Ritchie. Playgoers may also have been aware that when they stepped into the Moorish-style Casino, at 39th and Broadway, diagonally across from the old Metropolitan Opera House, they were walking into a small bit of theatrical history: when the theatre opened, nearly twelve years earlier in 1882, it was the first auditorium ever constructed in America purposely to house light musical entertainment.

Rosenfeld's text, despite the disclaimer in the *Times* that "Of course, there was no plot," did have a thread of a story connecting the songs and sketches, and thus set a pattern for the entire first generation of American revues. Many of the performers were assigned characters and played them, at least intermittently, throughout the evening. Rosenfeld created his story by extending his parody of a contemporary play so that it cropped up, off and on, until the last curtain. The play he parodied was Sydney Grundy's English success, *Sowing the Wind*, which had come to America only the preceding January. In it a man attempts to prevent his adopted son from marrying an undesirable girl, just as years before his own father had stopped him from making an unfortunate marriage. But the woman whom the older man had loved was a lady of dubious reputation, while the son's fiancée seemingly has a spotless name. In the end the younger girl turns out to be the daughter of the woman the father had turned away from. In Charles Frohman's original production (one block north at the Empire), Henry Miller had been Barbazon, the father; William Faversham, Ned, the son; and Viola Allen, Rosamond, the younger woman. In Rosenfeld's redaction it is Rosamond who is Barbazon's ward. His Barbazon (called Brabson in some programs) hires a detective to find sufficient evidence to prevent the marriage, and the detective's journeys through New York's byways provided the single thread that held the evening together. Although De Angelis portrayed the detective, he also found time and flimsy theatrical excuses to make comic appearances as Charley's Aunt, as the popular farceur, John Drew, as the author-playwright, James A. Herne, and even as the show's composer-conductor, Englander.

This summary hardly does full justice to the complications in Rosenfeld's story. For instance, another character, Haf Quickstep, escapes from a prison where he has been held on trumped-up charges. He disguises himself as an actor and joins a performance of an amateur theatrical at the Dawdle Club (which contemporaries saw as a spoof of the Vaudeville Club). It is during this performance that the detective assumes the guise of conductor, recognizes Quickstep, and stops the show to haul him off to court. At the Palace of Justice "tempered with mercy," Quickstep is defended by Rowe and Rummel, whom playgoers understood as Howe and Hummel, a leading pair of New York lawyers.

Nor was *Sowing the Wind* the only well-known theatrical work to be twitted. Rosenfeld also spoofed Arthur Wing Pinero's *The Amazons*, the wordless French pantomime *L'Efant Prodigue*, and Emma Calvé in *Carmen*. Opera in general was satirized in what many critics considered the evening's high point, a skit called "Round the Opera in Twenty Minutes," which used such whistled-to-death airs as "After the Ball," "Annie Rooney," and "The Man Who Broke the Bank at Monte Carlo" to ridicule the stylistic eccentricities of Bizet, Gounod, Leoncavallo, Verdi, and, most of all, Wagner. The then-famous Kilvan "living pictures" were travestied in comic tableaux. Adam and Eve were all but hidden behind enormous fig leaves, and Venus was seen rising not from the sea but from an 1894 bathtub. (There was something unintentionally appropriate about the presence of these tableaux showing the birth of mankind and the birth of a goddess in a revue that helped give birth to a new genre.)

Songs as well as skits had fun at the expense of contemporary theatre. As a rule songs of the day employed short, simple choruses, saving the meat of their arguments for a multiplicity of lengthy verses. Thus, "Old Before His Time" offered a drivelling, sixteen-bar chorus saying nothing except, "yes, that is one thing makes a man old before his time." But the second of its many verses took aim squarely at the new Ibsenite realism that was offending so many less adventuresome playgoers. It ran in part:

> *The heroine has consumption,*
>   *the hero meningitis.*
> *The villain, yellow jaundice;*
>   *oh, his sufferings are fearful.*
> *The scene's laid in a hospital,*
>   *to make it nice and cheerful;*

.   .   .

And the audiences are wading
thro' the mire and the slime,
As they feel themselves grow old
before their time.

Although the theatre of the day figured most importantly in the
songs and sketches, it was not Rosenfeld's sole concern. Coxey's Army
was given a song of its own. And then, of course, there was that staple
of all theatrical musicals, love. "I Love My Love in the Springtime"
may have been a more or less standard romantic number, but "Sex
Against Sex" was an early battle of the sexes which dealt with surprising
directness with illegitimacy and concluded that whatever the cause the
battle would continue "For aye and aye." (The song's title came from
the line that opened the "big" scene in Grundy's play.) Still, *The Passing
Show* set another pattern for the earliest revues by giving short shrift to
boy meets girl duets.

Despite advance ballyhoo and all the discussions of the musical's
provenance, critics were thrown into some disarray when they came to
assess the new work. The *Sun* saw it as an attempt to move away from
farce-comedy, a genre which by 1894 had evolved into musical comedy.
The *Times* headline ran "A Variety Show with Some Touches of Burlesque in It." Whoever composed the lead clearly had lifted his summary
from the unsigned review, which noted, "We do not know what a
topical extravaganza is; neither do they. That makes no difference. It
might as well have been called an articulated burlesque or a desiccated
variety show." Nearly a month later, the paper's principal critic, Edward
A. Dithmar, who may have been the opening night critic, reexamined
the show and concluded, "It goes well as a farrago of unrelated nonsense,
with a bit of clever travesty . . . and a great deal of downright 'variety
show' for good measure."

The *Times*'s bafflement about the meaning of "topical extravaganza"
is curious, unless one accepts it as a bit of snide smart-aleckry by a
second stringer. Topicality, as we have noted, was certainly nothing
new to the stage, and extravaganza had long been part of the New York

theatre scene, especially since 1866 when *The Black Crook* had set a new, lasting standard of lavishness for Broadway playgoers. What is far more interesting, though, is the failure of the *Times*'s critic, or most other critics for that matter, to devote any space to the sumptuousness of the show. From the moment of its opening the Casino had built a reputation for the opulence of its productions, a reputation that had long since spread nationwide and had prompted many New York visitors to attend a Casino production regardless of the musical being offered just to see for themselves the house's renowned excellence in mounting. Indeed, the Casino's chorus line was generally acknowledged as by far the most beautiful and attractively costumed in the country, and this fame held firm until later challenged first by Weber and Fields and then by Florenz Ziegfeld. Since there is no reason to believe that Lederer and his Casino staff stinted on *The Passing Show* nor that in fact the show did not continue the house's tradition of lavishness and taste, the omission by the critics of significant remarks on the musical's physical aspect is especially intriguing. To some extent it may simply mean that they were coming to take for granted the beauty of the Casino's mount-ings. (In their later years even Ziegfeld's splendors were sometimes passed over as if a matter of course.) But it may also suggest that, whether they realized it or not, the critics were far more attracted by the comedy and topicality, in short by the textual aspects of the show than by its sumptuousness. Their passing over of the songs suggests as much, too. The *Times* spoke merely of "a good deal of pretty music," while other papers drew on such contemporary critical standbys as "tinkly" and "reminiscent." This was, of course, not a great era for American show music. (Victor Herbert, the first truly enduring composer for our theatre, did not to make his debut until the next season.) Thus, the merely serviceable music, like the expected opulence, was relegated for the moment to a somewhat secondary position. The engaging satire and its attendant play of ideas apparently capped and justified the entertain-ment, and Rosenfeld thus set into motion the pattern for early American musical revue, in which a highly entertaining review of events would for many years take precedence over superior music, mounting, and just about everything else.

At least one number set some critics at loggerheads. The *Herald* insisted, "One of the best features of 'The Passing Show' was the ballet in the second act, when four dainty Phrynettes twirled around four Pierrots." Although the girls wore knee-high black stockings and knee-length black skirts, the shocked critic for the *Sun* reported, "The skirts were made of gauze so thin that the upper halves of their legs and lower halves of their bodies were plainly exposed in skin-tight, flesh-colored silk webbings" and he saw in these "a flagrant and shameful exploit in nudity" so "disgraceful" that "women averted their eyes and men were ashamed to look."

Even in the face of uncertain notices *The Passing Show* was a success, running into August (a good run at that time), and then embarking on a year-long tour which included a three-week return to the Casino in the fall and two shorter, later stands at other New York houses. In more ways than one the musical was the right show at the right time. First of all, it was viewed as a "summer show," the sort of light, frothy entertainment popular at that period to make playgoers forget the heat in un-airconditioned theatres. Second, it came at just the time when the first wave of European operettas and comic operas, the universally enjoyed works by Gilbert and Sullivan, Offenbach, Strauss, and others, had about run its course. Compared with preceding decades, European operetta was in the doldrums. Nor had American writers of operetta, with the dubious exceptions of Reginald DeKoven and Harry B. Smith, and perhaps the somewhat unappreciated John Philip Sousa, offered serious rivalry. The sui generis Harrigan and Hart musical plays had also had their day, as had American burlesques on the order of *Evangeline* and *Adonis*. American musical comedy, having but recently escaped the cocoon of farce-comedy, was still in its infancy and had produced only one resounding, if primitive, success, the 1891 *A Trip to Chinatown*. In the next season, along with the arrival of Herbert, came the premiere of *A Gaiety Girl*, the first of the imported English Gaiety Theatre musicals which brought a new sense of style, tone, and maturity to musical comedy and started that genre on its decades of established acclaim and vogue. So Lederer, Rosenfeld, Englander, and the Casino had offered Americans an exciting, potentially exploitable new genre right in the midst of a lull in musical theatre history and at a moment when Americans, first basking in their new-found prestige as citizens of a growing world power, were disposed to embrace anything fresh and home-made. "Up-to-date" and "Yankee made" were catch phrases of the era.

The success of *The Passing Show* was not so overwhelming that others rushed in with imitations. For several seasons the Casino had the field to itself. But the theatre persevered, even in the face of a near failure on its second try. That "Second Annual Summer Review," *The Merry World*, opened June 8, 1895, and played a mere four weeks. Nonetheless it kept alive both the idea of a revue and the notion that a revue was primarily a summer entertainment. Lederer and his some-times silent partner, Thomas Canary, gave over the writing of the show largely to two figures new to the genre—Edgar Smith, who was then embarking on what became a long career as a librettist and lyricist, and to a much respected composer-conductor, William Furst, whose musical comedy *The Little Trooper* had enjoyed a run at the Casino the preceding fall, and who was regularly called upon to compose incidental music for major Broadway dramas. The producers filled the cast with beloved oldtimers such as Amelia Summerville (a once notoriously fat comedienne who became one of the earliest advocates of strenuous dieting) and rising young talents such as David Warfield. But several things apparently went wrong. First of all, none of the cast possessed the box-office appeal of De Angelis or Ritchie. Second, whatever his prestige and skill, Furst was no better a melodist than Englander. Last, Smith made a timid retreat from the relatively tight, fully conceptualized approach of Rosenfeld. Slim as Rosenfeld's plotline had been, he had made some attempt to maintain it throughout *The Passing Show*. On the other hand, Smith merely suggested at the beginning of the revue that the audience would be taken on a theatrical tour and each of his three acts dealt almost entirely with satirizing a single play or type of entertainment. His first act parodied *Madame Sans-Gêne*; his second, the popular musicals of the day, including *Wang*, *Rob Roy*, and *Robin Hood*; while his last act, generally accounted the best, focused on *Trilby*. To add to the Casino's woes, five nights before its revue opened, a full-length burlesque called *Thrilby*, which even managed to incorporate a secondary spoof of *Madame Sans-Gêne*, had opened to great acclaim.

Canary and Lederer clearly learned the lessons from their near miss, so the following May, when they offered their "3rd Annual Review" (note the elimination of "summer"), they scored their biggest hit to date with *In Gay New York*. For lyricist-librettist they turned to Hugh Morton, who before his early death would become a leading librettist and who, under his real name, C. M. S. McLellan, was to write one of the finest of turn-of-the-century American dramas, *Leah Kleschna*. To compose the melodies they hired the theatre's new musical director, Gustave Kerker, who would later write with Morton *The Belle of New York*, an internationally applauded musical comedy. The cast was again filled with rising young performers, including not only Warfield, but Virginia Earle, Richard Carle, and Walter Jones.

Morton's plot, still admittedly slim, was nevertheless the most solid to date. It concerned a bride and groom, whose wedding opened the show, and followed them on their honeymoon to New York City, where they are almost waylaid at Grand Central Station by some "bunco-steerers" (a nineteenth-century term for con men), but are rescued in the nick of time by a group of traveling players who decide to show them the town. Inevitably the story leaned heavily on satirizing contemporary shows and celebrities. In this respect the evening could be perceived as little more than the umpteenth variation of the old Tom and Jerry motif, but the inventive Morton went much further. He emphasized romance to an extent his predecessors had not, including a number of simple love songs. He also introduced a note, heretofore missing, that would be given great prominence in many later revues—nostalgia. One scene purported to show the Casino after the audience had left a performance. When a night watchman turns out the lights a spirit summons the ghosts of old players who offer a history of the Casino's bygone hits until dawn and the scrubwomen arrive. Morton also returned to an older tradition by placing stooges in the audience for occasional scenes. The *Times*, slightly unhappy over his apparently excessive use of this device, still managed to put it into historical context when it complained of "a little too much of the very old Mitchell-Burton-Brougham 'business' of scattering performers around the auditorium and having them interrupt the stage performance." Before the newlyweds and their friends moved on to Coney Island for a grand finale, the audience had been regaled with a variety of songs such as "Girlie Girl," "The Cripple Creek Bandits," "It's Forty Miles from Schenectady to Troy," "Jusqu'la" (which spoofed French musical hall stars), "Lurline," "Molly," and "Trip Around the Town." It was a variety which suggested the fullness of interests of later revues and not the intra-theatrical concerns that had heretofore dominated such shows. One novelty, according to the *Herald*, was that several scene changes were made in full view of the audience. And on this occasion the *Sun*, which had taken umbrage over costumes in *The Passing Show*, reported with apparent relief that there were "no indecencies."

In Gay New York ran for 120 performances and toured for two years, making several profitable return trips to Broadway. The breadth of interest which Morton had shown could be displayed in a revue and the musical's rousing success prompted the imitations which *The Passing Show*'s modest success and *The Merry World*'s squeak-through run had not. In a sense, then, *In Gay New York* was as crucial, perhaps more so, in the subsequent flowering of the revue as *The Passing Show*. Moreover, another development took place which possibly assured that the American revue would not be narrowly theatrical in its interests and would thus appeal to ever-widening audiences.

On September 5, 1896, early in the season following *In Gay New York*'s premiere, Weber and Fields opened their music hall. Within a very short time this pint-sized theatre with its minuscule stage became the most chic of Broadway's musical houses, usurping in good measure the supremacy the Casino had enjoyed ever since it opened. While the music hall never offered revues per se, its influence on the genre, albeit indirect, was monumental. Weber and Fields soon developed a pattern for their programs that sustained them until the pair split. The program was essentially a double bill consisting of a long, if not quite full-length musical comedy coupled with an extended burlesque of the reigning Broadway hit of the moment. In the little less than the decade in which they flourished these burlesques were seen by contemporaries as the pinnacle of their kind, the most brilliant series of theatrical travesties the American stage had yet offered. Reputedly, when they became the rage of Broadway, producers offered bribes to Weber and Fields to mock their productions, since many playgoers insisted on seeing the original before attending the Weber and Fields spoof. In many instances not only were the plays hilariously twitted but their sets and costumes were imitated as precisely as the music hall's tiny stage would allow. Even the titles were fun, *The Geisha* evolving into *The Geezer*, and *Barbara Frietchie* becoming *Barbara Fidgety*. Two favorite ways in which they poked fun at plays were to turn the story inside out and to lard it with anachronisms. A good example is *Quo Vas Iss?*, their spoof of *Quo Vadis*, in which the Emperor Zero is horrified to learn that the W. C. T. U. is threatening to burn Rum. While the musical comedy ran out each season, the burlesques were replaced at intervals with newer burlesques of more recent openings. Only the bravest or most foolhardy of revue producers would attempt to challenge Weber and Fields, so revue writers were soon scurrying to discover other worlds to ridicule. With rare exceptions later revues would never again be so preoccupied with self-centered theatrical mocking as were the very first ones.

Weber and Fields also lured away some of the Casino's best performers, notably David Warfield and Lee Harrison. As a result the Casino and the other houses which soon jumped on the bandwagon were forced to look around for fresh talent. The explosive growth of the revue, which was in any case just around the corner, would have forced a similar search on its own, but Weber and Fields nonetheless initiated the rush.

A third point was the excellence of Weber and Fields physical mountings and the beauty of their chorus line, both of which rivaled and apparently often surpassed the Casino's. Precisely how superior these mountings were can now only be a matter for conjecture, but the important point is that critics, and undoubtedly audiences, of the day perceived a superiority. In the highly competitive world of theatre this almost certainly had to raise standards at other houses, perhaps even at the Casino.

The 1896-97 season also saw some other interesting developments that would eventually touch the revue. In the long run the most important was the producing debut of Florenz Ziegfeld, although he would not produce his first revue until 1907. Less directly significant was the opening of Victor Herbert's first major success, *The Serenade*. Herbert was to lead the way in elevating musical standards in the American theatre, standards which would eventually glorify the best American revues (and complete their special balance) as much as the great clowns, great wits, and Ziegfeld's beautiful girls.

If these influences on the American revue were sometimes indirect and not manifested immediately, the results of *In Gay New York*'s success bore fruit promptly. During late winter and early spring of the 1896-97 season three musicals appeared which were considered by at least some critics as revues, although two, *At Gay Coney Island* and *In Gayest Manhattan; or, Around New York in Ninety Minutes,* called themselves farce-comedies and the third, *Miss Manhattan,* was advertised as an extravaganza. Critics also called them vaudevilles and musical comedies. The confusion is easily explained. Many critics were still not certain of the basic differences between a vaudeville show and a revue, seeing both merely as kaleidoscopes of entertainments, while the thin plots associated with all revues of the era must have often made them indeed difficult to separate from some of the skimpily storied musical comedies (or farce-comedies, as certain primitive musical comedies were still called). That *In Gayest Manhattan* was presented at Koster and Bial's, a leading vaudeville house, no doubt exacerbated the confusion. In any case, all three failed.

More important, however, as far as *In Gay New York*'s success was concerned, was the fact that come season's end it spawned not one but two indisputable revues. For the first time the Casino found itself with real competition. And, as if to rub salt into the wound, the competitor, *A Round of Pleasure,* which was produced by Klaw and Erlanger of the notorious Theatrical Syndicate, was from the pens of *The Passing Show*'s authors, Rosenfeld and Englander. Although it, too, enlisted some of the rising young talents from the Casino's companies, the Casino's skills and reputation won the day. Its "fourth annual review," *The Whirl of the Town*, written again by Morton and Kerker, not only far outran the new rival but enjoyed a slightly longer stand than had *In Gay New York* or *The Passing Show.*

When the back-to-back successes of *In Gay New York* and *The Whirl of the Town* were followed by *Yankee Doodle Dandy*, a trouble-plagued, disappointing summer revue in 1898, the Casino backed off cautiously from continuing the series—at least as far as its main auditorium was concerned. But the house had been the first in America to erect an open-air theatre on its roof for hot-weather entertainment, and even before *Yankee Doodle Dandy* premiered, playgoers were climbing the stairs or taking the theatre's creaky elevators to the roof to see a show called *Rice's Summer Nights.*

E. E. Rice, a name now forgotten by all but the most devoted theatrical historians, was a landmark pioneer in the American musical. He had written and/or produced the long popular burlesque, *Evange-line*, and the record-breaking *Adonis*. He organized one of the first farce-comedy companies, Rice's Surprise Party, which figured importantly in the earliest development of native musical comedy. Along with Augustin Daly, he was one of the first American producers to import the turn-of-the-century West End musicals, which furthered the growth of musical comedy. Among the major performers he offered a vigorous leg-up were Henry E. Dixey, Lillian Russell, and Fay Templeton. Before he retired he would give an equally crucial helping hand to Julian Eltinge and to Jerome Kern. But by 1898 his career was drawing to a close. Nonetheless, he was still adventuresome. Contemporary notices suggest *Rice's Summer Nights* may have been closer to pure vaudeville than to revue. At this remove, with no text in hand, it is impossible to say. Although the title was employed week in, week out, much of the bill appears to have been changed regularly, there appears to have been no attempt to connect the acts with a plot, and the performers seem to have largely brought their own material with them. However, beginning on July 5, three weeks before the opening of *Yankee Doodle Dandy*, he added an afterpiece to the bill that set New York agog and remained a part of the show for much of the summer. That afterpiece was a musical playlet called *The Origin of the Cake Walk;*

or, *Clorindy*, and it was the first show written and performed by blacks ever to play a major Broadway house.

For the next decade revues appeared regularly if unexcitingly almost every season. To list examples is meaningful if only to show how meaningless the list is: *The Giddy Throng; The King's Carinval; Punch, Judy and Co.; A Little Bit of Everything*, and so on. Almost none were major successes—despite the occasional presence of important stars—and none left behind any major songs. The biggest hit of all came at the end of the decade when Lew Fields, having dissolved his partnership with Weber, produced *About Town* in 1906. While the mounting displayed the characteristics for which Fields had become known—superb sets and costumes, excellent staging, and a gorgeous chorus line, it represented no real progress. Another anorexic plot recounted the adventures of an English duke and a friendly New York cab driver as they tour the city until the Duke finally decides which of two girls he will marry. A star-filled cast included Lawrence Grossmith, Edna Wallace Hopper, Louise Dresser, Jack Norworth, Vernon Castle, Peter Dailey, Blanche Ring, and Fields himself. Although a long roster of composers, among them Gus Edwards, Raymond Hubbell, Kerker, and even Victor Herbert, collaborated on the score, nothing of enduring value emerged.

Precisely how many revues were produced in this period is moot, since the line between the plotted revues and the slap-dash musical comedies of the era was often impossible to discern. For example, the series of musicals starring the Rogers Brothers, a series mounted by the Syndicate (a largely successful producing and theatre-owning monopoly established by Abe Erlanger and his associates) to buck Weber and Fields's popularity, was generally advertised as musical comedy, but more than one critic called these shows revues. Tenuous plots took the "Dutch" dialect brothers, Gus and Max, on adventures in Washington, Harvard, and other romantic places, but were provided with enough holes to allow all manner of extraneous song and dance. Perhaps even more interesting was the case of *The Little Duchess*, which Ziegfeld had produced in 1901 for Anna Held, his wife at the time. Some touring programs contained the notice "Owing to the length of the performance the plot has been eliminated." Had a musical comedy been abruptly turned into the first modern plotless revue?

Several reasons can be suggested for the failure of the revue to develop more rapidly and more artistically. To begin with, it was exactly in this period that Victor Herbert revived interest in American operetta with such memorable works as *The Fortune Teller* and *Mlle. Modiste*. At the same time, American musical comedy (always allowing that we can be sure we are talking about musical comedy instead of revue) had been spurred by the example of the Gaiety shows. In New York, George M. Cohan had brought forth his tautly written, melody-filled shows such as *Forty-five Minutes from Broadway*, *Little Johnny Jones*, and *George Washington, Jr.* In Chicago, Joe Howard and his collaborators were doing much the same. New York also offered the gigantic Hippodrome's unique spectacles, exceptionally large-scale productions which straddled the fence between revue and book musical, once more using the flimsiest of story lines to transport audiences to wherever an eye-boggling setting could be offered—an imposing Oriental temple, a gigantic waterfall, a massive inferno. Added attractions ranged from horses diving into the theatre's huge tank, to the band of John Philip Sousa. As a result, revues, though now secure, were rather the waifs of our musical theatre. Matters began to change in 1907.

3

Ziegfeld and His Follies

Ziegfeld! The name still has a magic to it! Although he has been dead for well over half a century, there are probably not many Americans for whom his name will fail to conjure up visions of a very special glamour. How few theatrical figures of his time or earlier, whatever their theatrical concerns, have left behind a similar legacy. The Barrymores? Perhaps. Lillian Russell? At one time, yes; but increasingly less so. John Wilkes Booth occupies a unique, rather dishonored niche. Forrest, Edwin Booth, possibly Joseph Jefferson are the private preserve of theatrical historians, while Eugene O'Neill and several other playwrights and composers may still be alive for intellectuals. Ziegfeld is virtually alone in calling from the past to evoke a shimmering, glittering spell.

It was that way, to an extent, even in his lifetime once he had built his reputation. When, at the height of his career, he produced the great musical hit *Sally,* Alexander Woollcott exclaimed at the end of his notice, "It is of none of these, not of [Joseph] Urban, nor Jerome Kern, not of Leon Errol, not even of Marilynn Miller that you think first as you rush for the subway at ten minutes to midnight. You think of Ziegfeld. He is that kind of producer. There are not many of them in the world." One can only speculate on what other producers Woollcott might have had in mind and wonder how well they are remembered today. Seven years later, when the producer offered the original production of *Show Boat*, critic after critic perceived the musical not so much as Jerome Kern and Oscar Hammerstein's masterpiece but rather as Ziegfeld's. He was, indeed, that kind of producer.

Florenz Ziegfeld, Jr., was born in Chicago in March 1867 (sources disagree whether the date was the 15th or the 21st), the son of a locally well-known musician and pedagogue. He began to display his independence and eccentricity early on, although not in a manner suggesting his future distinction. When Florenz, Sr., was appointed director of musical events for the 1893 Columbian Exposition, he sent his young son to Europe to secure the finest contemporary talent. Instead of hiring the noted musical artists clearly his father had in mind, he signed contracts with a variety of music hall performers and circus acts. In the same year he became manager of the famed strongman Eugene Sandow. His imaginative promotion of his client, creating stunning, well-publicized effects for his act, gave the first clue of the path he would take. However, it was his marriage to Anna Held, his first wife (although there is some dispute as to whether they were, in fact, legally married), that firmly set him on the road to future greatness. To present her to Broadway he offered a revival of Charles Hoyt's farce-comedy, A *Parlor Match*. Of course, he starred the play's original comedians Charles Evans and William Hoey, but it was his presentation of the beautiful, coquettish singer, surrounded by a few lovely young ladies, all gorgeously gowned, that signaled his eventual course. Contemporaries and historians have suggested that it was another vehicle for Miss Held, the 1899 *Papa's Wife*, in which Ziegfeld utilized a much talked-about chorus of sixteen ravishing girls, that he first fully realized his genius. For the next eight years, with the exception of a mounting of DeKoven's operetta, *The Red Feather*, all his musical productions centered on Miss Held.

Both Miss Held and Ziegfeld agree that it was she who suggested to him the idea of his mounting a summer revue. The suggestion is interesting, since she must have been aware that neither New York nor London, where she had played for a time, had taken to the revue as wholeheartedly as had Paris or Berlin. But for all the American jingoism prevalent at the time, the couple astutely recognized the appeal of Continental traditions, especially to a well-heeled segment of sophisticated New Yorkers. Moreover, both may have been cognizant of the essential similarity of Broadway's summer theatrical roof gardens and the Continental cabaret-theatres where revues were flourishing. Turn-of-the-century roof gardens, although open-aired, can best be compared with those modern abominations, dinner-theatres. As in many dinner-theatres, audiences watched the show not crammed into narrowly tiered rows of small seats, but crowded around tables, where both food and beverages could be served all through the performance.

If, as some have claimed, Miss Held also suggested a name for the show, at least one first-hand authority has disputed the claim. The famous librettist and lyricist Harry B. Smith, who was to provide the libretto and lyrics for the first *Follies* and for four of the five succeeding editions, told a different story in his autobiography. According to Smith, in his newspaper days he had written a column called "Follies of the Day," so when he sat down to write the book for the new revue he not only recalled that title but, accepting the perception of the time that a revue was merely a review of the season's foibles, he offered the title *Follies of the Year.* As Smith remembered, the producer liked the basic idea but, recollecting that several of his hits had had thirteen letters in their titles, insisted on changing the name to *Follies of 1907.* (Curiously, Smith lists as examples two titles which have thirteen letters only if the article is omitted, *The Little Duchess* and *The Parisian Model,* and a third, *Miss Innocence,* which was not produced until several years later. By way of rebuttal, when the show was first advertised Ziegfeld did, indeed, place numbers over each letter to show that there were thirteen.) Ziegfeld also accepted the notion that a revue was a review, and in many advertisements, programs and sheet music used that spelling. Yet he was apparently of both turns of mind, for some programs and advertisements also spoke of "The Ziegfeld Musical Revue."

Because the Jamestown Centenary Exposition was in the news, Smith used Captain John Smith and Pocahontas as compère and commère, that is, as master and mistress of ceremonies. To the extent that this pair served solely in those capacities, Smith was making a distinct bow to the French tradition of using a host or hostess instead of a plot to tie together innumerable loose ends. Virtually no other American revue, quite possibly none if a careful study of texts could be made, had used this device. However, Smith played it both ways for safety, also incorporating the couple in a most transparent return-to-life-for-modern-tour-of-the-city story. Tom and Jerry were still very much alive.

The twentieth-century celebrities Captain Smith and Pocahontas encountered included President Theodore Roosevelt, "wearing his Rough Rider uniform and displaying a spectacular array of teeth"; the famous politician and orator, Chauncey Depew, whom Smith placed in charge of a "Misinformation Department"; the would-be arbiter of all public morals, Anthony Comstock; tycoons Andrew Carnegie and John D. Rockefeller; the noted explorer Commodore Peary; and Mark Twain, who was called "Easy Mark." Hewing closer to the theatre, Smith also brought in Oscar Hammerstein and Heinrich Conried—who fought an operatic duel over their competing opera companies—John Philip Sousa, actress Edna May, and many others, including Enrico Caruso—who was tried on stage (by a jury of twelve beauties) for his then famous antics at the Central Park monkey house, where he is reputed to have pinched a young lady. The songs, penned in this instance not by a single composer and single lyricist but by a multiplicity of hands, gave further indications of the wide variety of themes and settings brought to life: "As You Walk Down the Strand," "Be Good! (If You Can't Be Good, Be Careful)," "Budweiser's a Friend of Mine" (the beer company reputedly helped underwrite the cost of the number), "Bye Bye Dear Old Broadway," "Handle Me with Care," "How'd You Like To Take Me Home with You," "I Think I Oughtn't Auto Anymore," "Miss Ginger from Jamaica," "The Modern Sandow Girl," "On the Grand Old Sand," and "Reincarnation."

Ziegfeld had long been allied with Klaw and Erlanger's Syndicate, so when he was ready to mount the new show they not only bankrolled it for him but redecorated the roof garden that sat atop the New York Theatre and spilled over to the roof of the adjoining Criterion. The space was redesigned to capture the flavor of a French cabaret-theatre and was renamed, appropriately, Jardin de Paris. The show opened on July 8. The cost of the original production was $13,000, an unexceptional figure at the time. Running costs have been given variously as anywhere from $1,800 to $4,000 per week, with the latter figure probably somewhere nearer the truth.

What Ziegfeld thought of Smith's libretto cannot be known for certain, but obviously he was aware that not only was Smith the most productive librettist (and lyricist) of the era, he was also one of the most highly respected. Nevertheless, Ziegfeld assuredly saw Smith's work as merely a skeleton requiring ample fleshing out. He must have known he had to put his own stamp on it, and immediately set about doing so. To this end he hired four directors: the respected Herbert Gresham to work with the principal performers, and Joe Smith, John O'Neil, and Julian Mitchell to stage the ensemble numbers.

Smith and O'Neil were minor figures, Mitchell was not. Mitchell, a nephew of the beloved actress Maggie Mitchell, had learned pacing under the watchful eye of Charles Hoyt, whose *A Trip to Chinatown* was then the longest running musical comedy in Broadway history and would remain so for a dozen more years. After leaving Hoyt, Mitchell became director for Weber and Fields, who, as we have seen, were the leading turn-of-the-century musical producers. In some ways Mitchell was an oddity. Although virtually his whole career was spent staging musicals, he had become almost totally deaf and, according to rumor, what little music he could hear left him indifferent. Ziegfeld, too, was long said to be unconcerned about the songs that filled his shows, but the record of enduring melodies that came from his *Follies* and his other shows belies this. But if Mitchell lacked one sense seemingly vital to a musical's director, his feel for pacing and his eye for beauty were second to none, not even Ziegfeld's. One immediate result was that the reputation for having Broadway's most eye-popping chorus line, which, having passed from the fading Casino to the now shuttered Weber and Fields' Music Hall, almost instantly and irrevokably attached itself to the *Follies*. As if to assure this, Ziegfeld called his chorus the Anna Held Girls, thus imparting to them some of his wife's exotic allure. There is some dispute about the number of girls in the original edition—advertisements claimed fifty, but no surviving photographs confirm this. And he chose a famous young beauty, Annabelle Whitford, to head the line. Working with Mitchell, he marched the girls up and down the aisles as they played on snare drums in "I Want To Be a Drummer Boy," and also set up a miniature pool for a bathing beauty scene, "The Gibson Bathing Girls." In this last number Miss Whitford shocked some of the stuffier playgoers by her appearance in stockings and bloomers. One prophetic rhyme from the lyric of "The Modern Sandow Girl" promised, "The charm she discloses / By statuesque poses, must set ev'ry brain in a whirl."

Oddly enough, in a 1907 interview Ziegfeld seemingly made no mention of his girls. Instead he spoke casually of the new show as a "midsummer diversion," adding merely that it was "a satire on everything timely that has a burlesque side." (Seven years later an advertisement for the 1914 *Follies* suggested the producer's notion had not changed all that much. Above the title the revue was called "The One Established Summer Show"—no doubt a dig at the Shuberts' new series, while immediately below the title a line read "The Laughing Success." Only on the next line did he add "With All Its Pretty Girls.")

Another result of Mitchell's excellent work was that, although Ziegfeld rehired Gresham for the second edition, he made Mitchell his right-hand man and retained him as such for all but one of the *Follies* up to and including the 1915 edition. Ziegfeld was not so lucky at first in enlisting other associates. Costumes were by W. H. Matthews, Jr. and Mme. E. S. Freisinger; sets by Peter V. Griffin, T. Bernard McDonald, and John H. Young. Of these, only Young had more than a journeyman reputation. Better costume designers would appear shortly, but not until 1915 would he find the ideal set designer.

Like Miss Whitford, no other members of the cast went on to the truly legendary stature accorded later *Follies* performers. The best known were probably the principal prima donna, Grace LaRue, and the deep-voiced vaudeville belter, Emma Carus. The popular ballerina Mlle.

Dazie offered her version of "The Dance of the Seven Veils," a doll
dance, and a Jiu-Jitsu waltz, performing the last with a dancer billed
as Prince Tokio. Of the veil number the *American* observed, "Mlle.
Dazie performed her dance with all the grace and abandon that characterized Mlle. Froelich's performance in 'Salome' at the Metropolitan." (The reviewer also reported something no other paper seems to
have noticed—that the police raided the theatre as soon as the dance
was finished and arrested the dancer.) The comic team of Bickel and
Watson, and a normally Chicago-based funmaker, Dave Lewis, provided much of the laughter, although a promising young lady, who
later kept her promises, was widely applauded. She was Helen Broderick.

Not sensing an event of great importance, several newspapers, including the usually thorough *Times*, gave the opening scant notice and
no real review. Others, one important trade sheet among them, relegated
their criticism to their vaudeville sections. Regardless of where the
reviews were placed, most were anything but ecstatic. One critic, preoccupied with the Continental aspects of the show, took a typical public
Yankee attitude of the time: "In seeking to reproduce some of the
audacities of the French captial, Mr. Ziegfeld has come occasionally
into collision with a sense of propriety which distinguishes a large
portion of the public over here." A majority of critics found the evening
a mixture of entertaining highspots and dull moments. The aisle-sitter
who observed, "Mr. Ziegfeld has given New York the best melange of
mirth, music, and pretty young girls that has been seen here in many
summers," found few colleagues agreeing with him.

Nor were playgoers overwhelmed. To whet their interest Ziegfeld
advertised that many of the acts were changed weekly. As colder weather
approached toward the end of the nine-week run, Ziegfeld moved the
show into the more traditional, enclosed Liberty Theatre, also adding
Nora Bayes as a major attraction. Just how successful the New York
run was is uncertain. Historians writing about the show, almost to a
man, have insisted that it realized only modest returns but scored so
heavily in a brief tour of Washington and Baltimore that Ziegfeld wound
up with a $120,000 profit. As it stands, the claim is patently absurd,
since musicals of the era, when a $1.50 and sometimes $2.00 top

prevailed, generally grossed between $10,000 and $15,000 at capacity. Even with low, pre-union overheads Ziegfeld could not possibly have netted $120,000 in three months. What has been overlooked is that the show had a far more extensive tour, for example, opening at Philadelphia's Forrest Theatre on December 30, 1907, and remaining there until February 8, 1908. It was this prolonged, hugely successful post-Broadway journey that contributed most of the profits and determined Ziegfeld to make his revue an annual affair.

During the seven editions from 1908 through 1914 Ziegfeld steadily refined his art and enhanced his reputation. Although the producer did not coin his famous slogan, "Glorifying the American Girl," until 1922, when both the artistry and the popularity of the *Follies* had begun to wane, it was almost certainly the perception that these revues were the consummate "girlie shows" that was uppermost in the minds of many playgoers. Whatever the number of girls parading in the first edition, the figure soon rose to about sixty girls in each production, with a few offering seventy-five or eighty beauties in the line. Names such as Lillian Lorraine, Justine Johnstone, Marion Davies, Mae Murray, Jessie Reed, Olive Thomas, and the patronymicless Dolores, now mostly forgotten, were all but household words, and their escapades, sometimes true, sometimes invented, sometimes happy, sometimes tragic, were regularly in the headlines. On stage, their arch, haughty, chin-up strut set a new standard not only for the chorus lines of other revues but for parading mannequins everywhere.

However well-known Emma Carus may have been in 1907, it was with the hiring of Nora Bayes during the first edition's run that Ziegfeld embarked on another policy, employing the greatest stars of his era to add their unique glitter and excitement to his productions. Perhaps "employing the greatest stars" is somewhat inaccurate, for many of the names that soon shone most brightly in Ziegfeld's unique firmament were merely promsing young talents when Ziegfeld first hired them. To an extent this was true of Miss Bayes, but it applied even more to such later legendary performers as Fanny Brice, Eddie Cantor, Leon Errol, W. C. Fields, Marilyn Miller, Will Rogers, John Steel, and Ed Wynn. Other producers may have discovered them, but it was Ziegfeld

who put them on the theatrical map. One curious, important exception
was Bert Williams. This great black comedian had long since made a
name for himself in black musical comedies, but these musicals were
virtually sui generis mountings which the prejudices of the time con-
fined to small runs, usually only in major cities. In his unprecedented
hiring of Williams, Ziegfeld broke the centuries-old color barrier and
allowed a significant black artist to appear for the first time in a regular,
white musical. The year was 1910.

In the second edition of the *Follies* Nora Bayes introduced "Shine
On, Harvest Moon," thereby beginning another tradition—the introduction of enduring song hits in these revues. Ziegfeld's supposed indifference to the music in his shows is, as noted earlier, a matter of
record, but a record almost certainly exaggerated to serve others' ends.
Coupled with the realization that all earlier revues had produced prac-
tically nothing of lasting note, the list is not unimpressive, including
as it does, "By the Light of the Silvery Moon" (1909), "Row, Row,
Row" (1912), "Hello, Frisco" (1915), "Mandy" (1919), "A Pretty Girl
Is Like a Melody" (1919), "You'd Be Surprised" (1919), "Tell Me,
Little Gypsy" (1920), "Second Hand Rose" (1921), "My Man" (1921),
"Mr. Gallagher and Mr. Shean" (1922), "Chansonette" [source of "The
Donkey Serenade"] (1923), and "Shaking the Blues Away" (1927). If
this list is not quite as awesome as those from the *Scandals* or several
individual later revues, that may reflect in a small way the fact that text
and, in Ziegfeld's case and day, visual matters were still judged prime
considerations. The proper place of music in attaining a true sense of
balance for the American revue was slow in coming. Nonetheless,
wittingly or otherwise, it was Ziegfeld in his *Follies* who saw that the
earlier imbalance was finally redressed.

But then traditional textual ties were almost as slow in fading away.
For example, the 1908 *Follies* substituted Adam and Eve for Captain
Smith and Pocahontas, then went on yet another tour of the town. The
1911 edition, the first to incorporate Ziegfeld's name in the title, began
with *Follies* performers debarking from a ship. While going through
customs they sang songs in praise of New York, asked about and learned
about events while they were abroad, and in one manner or another

used their arrivals as cues for the various scenes. Echoing Brougham's long forgotten *Row at the Lyceum*, the 1912 *Follies* began with supposed members of the audience—all, of course, performers—interrupting the opening scenes to suggest those scenes did not represent the kind of production they had in mind. Their suggestions and complaints reappeared intermittently throughout the evening as an increasingly fragile link. By 1916, when more adventuresome revues had abandoned any pretense of plot, that year's edition of the *Follies* offered a "theme"—in this case, Shakespeare and his plays—to give a shaky semblance of unity to the evening.

The 1911 *Follies* offered one of the series' comic masterpieces, a skit some programs called "Upper and Lower Level." In it a jittery tourist, played by Leon Errol, arrives at Grand Central Station, where he enlists the services of a redcap, played by Bert Williams. Because of subway construction the pair must maneuver some girders, so Williams ties himself to Errol with a rope. Just as they are passing over a spot marked by a warning sign, "160 Foot Drop," Errol slips and falls. With an arduous hand-over-hand pull Williams brings Errol back up. But before he can secure firm footing Errol asks Williams for a match to light a pipe. Dutifully Williams rummages through his pocket while Errol plunges back down. Later Errol knocks over Williams's lunch pail, but apologizes by assuring Williams he will give him a nickel tip. Williams's withering look so unnerves Errol that he once again loses his balance. This time Williams, muttering "five cents," slowly releases the rope, then throws Errol's baggage after him. An explosion rises from the construction site below. Williams notes that Errol has been sent flying: "There he goes, now he's near the Metropolitan Tower. If he kin only grab that little gold ball on the top . . . 'um, he muffed it." Williams stares out at the audience with tongue-in-check regret.

Williams and Errol teamed up again in the next edition with equally memorable and hilarious results. In this instance Errol was a wobbly, inebriated tourist trying to hail a cab on Herald Square. (The *Herald*, not surprisingly, was delighted with the night setting, showing the newspaper's building busily lit.) The broken-down cab he picks has Williams as its shabby driver and is pulled by Nicodemus (played by two men), "the oldest livin' horse in New York." The horse is even wobblier than Errrol and has a way of lying down and crossing its legs when it senses real work. Much of the comedy came from Williams's attempts to keep both his fare and his horse from collapsing. In the end, the tourist, bidding the driver goodnight, falls asleep in the cab, and Williams, recognizing he can earn some not very honest bucks by driving his sleeping rider around, promises, "Oats, Nicodemus, OATS." The horse ambles off.

Visually, the *Follies* apparently improved with each edition, but it remains interesting, after a careful reading of reviews, to note that when, for example, a *Times* headline proclaims, " 'FOLLIES OF 1912' IS A BEAUTY SHOW," the beauty spoken of is usually that of the girls and their costumes. Thus, while the critic noted, "not the least pictorially lovely effects of the present show are produced in the final act, with the scene representing the interior of a curtain tent," his several paragraphs devoted to the stage picture continued in part:

> The scene, "The Palace of Beauty," brought a succession of lovely pictures. The audience gasped for one thing at the first figure to enter— a harlequin in a complete attire of thin black lace (Evelyn Hart). She was followed by a Venus (Elise Hamilton), whose graceful lines were admirably posed during a succession of other surprising revelations. Of these none was more alluring than the Duchess of Devonshire (Marie Baxter), a piquant blonde, to contrast with La Pompadour (Marion Hale) and Recamier (Katheryn Smyth).

The girls, their costumes, the comics, and an occasional song had been the mainstays of the *Follies* from the start and would continue to be so for two more years. Then, in 1915, a major change occurred.

The change was Joseph Urban. Urban was an Austrian, born in 1872 in Vienna, where he studied at the Art Academy and under Baron Carl Hassauer at the Polytechnicum. In 1904 he made his first trip to America, when he was commissioned to design the Austrian Pavilion for the St. Louis Fair. Seven years later the Boston Opera Company called him back to design some of its sets, but it was his work on the 1914 Broadway production, *The Garden of Paradise*, which brought him to Ziegfeld's attention. Although he was to design sets for other New York plays, to illustrate children's books, and to work on several private mansions and public buildings, as well as to be the primary designer for the great Ziegfeld Theatre, it was his work in Ziegfeld musicals for which he is largely remembered. From the moment his first *Follies* designs bedazzled 1915 audiences, the series (as well as all the Ziegfeld book musicals for which he created the sets) boasted a special quality, a unique opulence, stylishness and glamour that possibly more than anything set them apart from all other contemporary musicals and indeed from all succeeding ones. Somehow the unfailingly awesome beauty of his scenery—and "unfailing" and "awesome" were just two of many adjectives critics groped for in an attempt to express their seemingly swooning reactions—goaded Ziegfeld to elevate his standards for every other aspect of his productions. Although a number of earlier costumes, such as Evelyn Hart's thin, black-lace harlequin in 1912, had been singled out for description and praise, most of the costumes theretofore had simply been fancier or more gimmicky than in rival mountings. The black lace outfit represented the fancier creations while girls parading as fruits or as battleships exemplified the gimmicks. Ziegfeld abandoned neither after Urban's arrival, but he instantly understood that Urban's consummate designs required more artful complements. Virtually all of the classic costumes for which *Follies* are recalled were shown against Urban backgrounds.

Urban's detractors dismissed him as a "colorist," pouncing on one of his salient virtues while neglecting how his original sense of color was mated with the freshness and regal elegance of his sense of line and balance. Before Urban's appearance stage settings, especially in musicals, generally had been splashy kaleidoscopes of the gaudiest hues. Sets of carefully coordinated, subtly graded shades were so rare that critics often spent whole paragraphs extolling them when they were seen. But for some reason designers and producers took little heed of this attention, probably concluding that audiences paid more notice to bright crimson reds and sun-burst yellows on stage than they did to critics' encomiums in print.

From the start, however, Urban not only carefully coordinated his colors within a single set but often just as diligently planned the most selective evolution of colors from one setting to the next. Theatrical exigencies, which required rearranging the order of numbers after plans had been laid, frequently destroyed Urban's progressions but in no way diminished the intelligence of his initial conception.

An extraordinarily punctillious craftsman, Urban brought to the execution of his ideas the same singular thoroughness and artistry. After the initial pencil sketch, in which projected color placement was noted, he prepared a series of full color sketches. Once these were approved he built precisely tinted, foot-high pasteboard models. (Many of these— pencil sketches, color sketches, and models—survive in all their pristine beauty in the library of Columbia University.) To create the actual sets he worked with his canvases on the floor in order to allow an exact, firm application of paint. This in itself was not unknown, but Urban's next step was. For his method of painting was *pointillage*, in which rather than apply large, solid swathes of color he dappled small splotches of color side by side to give a more subtle effect from the distant auditorium. Audiences who may not yet have heard of Georges Seurat and his school of French painting, or who might still have been uneasy in the presence of Seurat's work in a museum, unhesitatingly and unquestioningly accepted Urban's breathtaking theatrical examples. One of Ziegfeld's biographers, Charles Higham, gives a specific example: "For a moonlit window casement he would have the background flat but well rubbed in. Next he applied with a finer brush a multitude of narrow green mottlings, like irregular ribbons. Over this he splattered a stipple of brick red. The casement turned gray-black under an amber light."

Accentuating Urban's remarkable eye for color was his sense of line and balance. Time and again his stage pictures were brilliantly composed and framed. For example, in the 1915 edition, the most famous set offered two trellised niches, one on each side of the stage, with each niche housing a huge, green-stuffed vase. The picture they framed disclosed a pair of huge elephants, trunks raised to the upper curtain line. From their trunks water poured into a lovely, circular pool behind which a typical Ziegfeld staircase climbed toward heaven. Another setting for the same edition, a superb bird's-eye view of London, over which a Zeppelin flew, was framed in a palatial window, complete with a lion in one corner and a gargoyled water spout in the other. Both Ziegfeld and Urban claimed blue was their favorite color, and their first joint venture was publicized as a "Blue Follies," with a blue underwater scene to open the show. Of course, the idea of doing an entire revue in shades of a single color was much too advanced for the time, as Ziegfeld and Urban both understood. So while, for instance, the London scene was largely in brown—with blue shadings, another scene, "My Radium Girl," relied on dramatic contrasts of white against black, and a patriotic number was done in red, white, and blue. A "Blue Follies" meant merely that blue would be the dominating color without in any way monopolizing the entertainment.

There was a rich ornateness to much of Urban's work, an ornateness of the Beaux Arts school, then still in vogue and which fitted in precisely with the grandiose baroque decorations of the New Amsterdam Theatre. (This gorgeous auditorium had sealed the primacy of 42nd Street as New York's principal theatre street when the house was opened in 1903, and by playing host to such prestigous hits as *The Merry Widow* had developed a cachet of its own by the time the *Follies* were moved there in 1913.) But Urban's work also displayed more modern influences, first of the curlicued simplifications of Art Nouveau, and second and more progressively, of the streamlining of Art Deco, although the latter was not to gain worldwide recognition and a name until the *Follies* had virtually run their course.

The 1915 *Follies*, besides its long line of gorgeous girls, included an awesome array of unforgettable talents, albeit some of them were only beginning to make their names known. Among performers held over from earlier editions were three exceptional clowns, Leon Errol, Bert Williams, and Ed Wynn. Who came off best depended largely on what style of buffoonery appealed to a particular playgoer. Critics gave wobbly-kneed Errol the shortest shrift. Williams had them rolling in the aisles in a sketch called "Hallway of the Bunkem Court Apartments," in which he portrayed the superintendent and switchboard operator. When one tenant advised him she was not at home to anyone, he asked, in that lugubrious innocence which masked a knowing cynicism, "Even the old gentleman?" Confusing similar sounding words just beyond his normal vocabulary, he inadvertently hit on the probable truth when he told a caller that another young lady had just left with "her fie-nance-eer." Wynn, sitting in a seat among the audience, attempted to direct a silent film in which singer Bernard Granville was to be the hero, beautiful Mae Murray the heroine, and Errol the villain.

Two newcomers to the series won special applause. Pert Ina Claire joined Granville to introduce the show's hit, "Hello, Frisco," celebrating the inauguration of transcontinental phoning, and also sang "Marie Odile," a mischievous ditty which slyly spoofed the heroine, an erring nun, in David Belasco's hit of the same name. Less subtle but equally irresistible were the antics of the other debutant, "an expert juggler with a sense of humor," W. C. Fields. His best moment came as a billiard player in a game made increasingly frustrating and frantic by warped and recalcitrant cues that seemed to have minds of their own. As Fields played or juggled he offered his audience some interesting biographical bits. He was, he told them, called "Honest John," a nickname earned after he found a glass eye and selflessly returned it to its owner.

Composer Louis Hirsch offered not only his long-lived San Francisco number but two songs which afforded Ziegfeld superior opportunities to parade his line and which enjoyed some contemporary popularity. Helen Rook sang the romantic "Hold Me in Your Loving Arms" while Granville, backed by a succession of appropriately dressed mannequins, warbled "A Girl for Each Month of the Year." Two fast-rising luminaries, Ann Pennington and George White, led the dancing.

Yet for all the superb performers and contributors, more than one critic proclaimed Urban the real "star" of the 1915 show.

The edition also marked the effective farewell to the series of Julian Mitchell, although he would return nine years later for one more time. To replace him Ziegfeld hired Ned Wayburn, a man twenty years Mitchell's junior, whose instincts for pacing and other theatrical requirements clearly reflected the changing tastes and tempos of the day.

Significantly, Wayburn is generally credited with inventing tap dancing, with its steely sounds and its faster rhythms mirroring the speedier machine age flourishing outside the theatre and the jazz age about to explode both inside and out.

Students have generally come to agree that the *Follies* reached their zenith with the eight editions from 1915 through 1922 and that the ultimate pinnacle came with the 1919 edition. Certainly critics and playgoers thought the 1919 edition was never equalled. The banners of New York newspapers told the story, with the *American* proclaiming "1919 'Follies' Surpasses All Others" and the *Herald* rejoicing "Thirteenth 'Ziegfeld Follies' Eclipses Predecessors in Beauty, Color and Action." The *Evening Sun* topped the general celebration by observing "Ziegfeld Outziegfelds Ziegfeld." Looking back, historian Robert Baral called the edition "a legend of perfection in show business."

Even on paper the show had as much as one could ask of a revue. The cast included Marilyn Miller, Eddie Cantor, Johnny Dooley, Ray Dooley, Van and Schenck, Bert Williams, Eddie Dowling, and John Steel, along with a list of Ziegfeld beauties headed by the Fairbanks Twins and Jessie Reed. A good part of the score was by Irving Berlin, whose work was supplemented by several other composers, including Victor Herbert. Of course, Urban and Wayburn were back. Happily, what looked so wonderful on paper looked just as good or better on stage when the musical opened at the New Amsterdam on June 16.

By the post-World-War-I era, writers and producers had abandoned plots and themes. The revue had reached the form with which it would be identified for almost all its remaining years, at best a lively, melodic juxtaposition of song, dance and comedy, with a large does of spectacle often thrown in. But the 1919 edition had a sort of running gag or theme popping up through it almost by accident, since revues were still looked on as important purveyors of topical satire, and this edition had raised its curtain just over two weeks before the advent of an overriding national concern—the beginning of Prohibition. A minor comedian named Phil Dwyer was dressed as a dog and performed a humorous skit showing how man's best friend would suffer along with his master. Eddie Cantor, trying to put a cheerful face on matters, sang "You Don't

Need the Wine To Have a Wonderful Time (While They Still Make Those Beautiful Girls)," but Bert Williams, who always saw life's more somber side in his uniquely humorous way, suggested (with Irving Berlin's help) "You Cannot Make Your Shimmy Shake on Tea." Even those beautiful girls whom Cantor sang about and whom Ziegfeld exploited so glamorously paraded to the strains of another Berlin number called "Prohibition." They paraded in "A Saloon of the Future," representing such liquid refreshers as Sarsaparilla, Grape Juice, Lemonade, Bevo, and Lady Alcohol. Not everyone was pleased by this probable overkill or by the various attempts to milk so much humor from a single event. The *Times*'s dour John Corbin felt the *Follies*' stabs at Prohibition, like those in other revues of the time, were not very laughable. But he hastily added that this reservation aside, the show set "a new mark for its superlative kind," and he tried to be objective by reporting "the high spots in the production, at least from the point of view of the audience, were touched by the comedians."

Foremost among these was Cantor's visit to an osteopath, a skit, he agreed, not "equalled in physical humor since the old days of Weber and Fields." In the skit Cantor portrayed the milquetoast Percival Fingersnapper, who comes to the doctor after being struck by a trolley. The rough pounding he receives at the doctor's hands convinces him being hit by a streetcar is not so bad after all. Cantor also had a show-stopping Berlin number, "You'd Be Surprised." (The song became so popular that, in a not uncommon practice of the time, it was soon being interpolated into at least two other Broadway musicals.) In this comparatively slow number, Cantor underscored the lyric's rather obvious humor by rolling his banjo eyes and by casting knowing glances at the audience. The jumpier, hand-clapping style (complete with the handkerchief-waving exit) with which he was so often associated was reserved for faster tunes. Williams, in what was to prove his last *Follies*, was not as lucky as Cantor. Apart from his "Shimmy" song, his material was judged inferior, and his success was a triumph of personality and comic genius. Ray Dooley played the incorrigible brat for which she was famous and, just to prove Williams unduly pessimistic, did a wild Shimmy. Other comic interludes, some musical, some not, spoofed everything from the rudeness of waiters, taxi drivers, and servants to the incessant comings and goings of President Wilson.

Spectacle began with the opening number, "The Follies Salad," in which the girls paraded as Lettuce, Spice, Oil, Chicken, Vinegar, Salt and Pepper, among others, and concluded with a finale which extolled the Salvation Army and offered Jessie Reed (whose salary of $125 per week was approaching that of the stars) as the Spirit of the Salvation Army. The first act finale was a glorified minstrel show, with Cantor and Williams as endmen and Marilyn Miller clog-dancing in the fashion of George Primrose. It was in this scene that Van and Schenck sang "Mandy." In between there were two sumptuous Ben Ali Haggan tableaux, "Hail to the Thirteenth Folly" and the medieval "Melody, Fantasy and Folly of Years Gone By." One other lavish scene, which remarkably few critics bothered to take note of, had girls sauntering on and off stage dressed to represent musical forms: for example, Martha Pierce portraying "Elegy," Alta King, "Serenade," and Jessie Reed, "Barcarolle." As they strolled, John Steel clarified the message of the number by singing the most famous song to come out of the *Follies*, one that might well have been its theme song, Berlin's "A Pretty Girl Is Like a Melody." However, it was another of Steel's appearances that many critics saw as one of the two high points of beauty in the evening, his singing with DeLyle Alda of "Tulip Time" as they meet in a Dutch garden beside a windmill and a dike. This scene vied for honors with a set depicting giant urns and flower bouquets in which Marilyn Miller danced "Sweet Sixteen."

The show opened at a time when postwar inflation was beginning to tell. Reputedly it cost well over $100,000 (some say over $150,000) at a time when *Irene*, a more typical production, cost $40,000. In the next year Ziegfeld would claim the 1920 edition went past the $200,000 mark. Stanley Green records that weekly expenses averaged $20,000 (or more than *Irene* grossed each week). Yet even at a $3.50 top Ziegfeld apparently made a respectable profit.

No evidence survives to suggest that Ziegfeld sensed that creeping inflation was one of several ominous developments which shortly were to doom his order of extravaganza or that its fall would be far more rapid than its rise. Of course, inflation alone would probably not have done in these magnificent mélanges. Our more recent, and more heinous, inflation demonstrated that there long remained an audience for quality entertainment at almost any price. But other developments followed thick and fast, and for all his theatrical acumen Ziegfeld was unable to override them.

The 1919 *Follies* had been running less than two months when Cantor, Miss Dooley, Steel, and Van and Schenck joined in the Actors' Equity strike, thus forcing the show to suspend. The union's demands at the time were largely reasonable, seeking in the main to protect performers from the callous treatment they had long and often received from the more greedy unprincipled producers. And even though Equity and other unions did not become overbearing and their demands outrageous until after Ziegfeld's death, they began to chip away at the prerogatives that allowed a producer of Ziegfeld's ilk to provide such lavish, abundant entertainment at a cost playgoers would accept and from which the producer could still hope for an acceptable return.

Actually Ziegfeld's own backstage ethics were not the best. It is generally believed, for example, that both Harry B. Smith and Julian Mitchell left him after feeling shortchanged on royalties, and even some of his stars were occasionally kept waiting for their salaries. (Years later Jerome Kern threatened to close *Show Boat* if his royalties were not forthcoming.) Moreover the demands Ziegfeld supposedly made on some of his more beautiful women were widely bruited about. One result of all this was that for longer or shorter periods, some of Ziegfeld's biggest stars abandoned him.

Broadway musicals were changing, too—especially revues. As we will see in the next two chapters, more intimate, liveliver, and often shorter revues were quickly coming into vogue. The more cynical, faster paced jazz musical comedies, which hit Broadway with a vengeance when *Lady, Be Good!* opened in 1924, dealt Ziegfeld a further blow. These musicals, as did much of "sophisticated" America of the time, effected a lean, tough, anti-romantic stance. Ziegfeld's leisurely (though never really slow-moving), gargantuan offerings were coming to be perceived as lumbering dinosaurs. His unstinting largesse (legend had it he insisted even unseen costume linings be made of the costliest materials) was viewed as overstuffed Victorian excess. And, indeed, at heart, for all their lightly debunking comedy and Tin Pan Alley style songs, the *Follies* were far more aligned in spirit if not in substance with roseate, sentimental operettas of an earlier time than they were with the brittle new revues and razor-sharp musical comedies.

But these perceptions were slow in developing. Certainly most critics found little to complain about in the 1920 and 1921 editions, the latter offering some of the series' most memorable moments thanks in no small measure to the star many considered Ziegfeld's greatest discovery, Fanny Brice. In the 1920 edition she had introduced two of her best comic songs, "I Was a Florodora Baby" ("Five little dumbbells got married for money / And I got married for love") and "I'm an Indian," celebrating her accomplishments as a squaw with a marked Yiddish accent. That Yiddish accent came in handy again in 1921 when she first presented another gem, half comic, half pathetic, "Second Hand Rose." But it was a second musical number from the edition which became the song always identified with her, the French "My Man." She sang it without a trace of accent, leaning against a lamp post and dressed like a tattered gamine. Originally the song was supposedly slated for a different singer. However, Ziegfeld recognized not only Miss Brice's more serious gifts but also, somewhat cynically, that her much publicized troubles with her worthless gangster husband, Nicky Arnstein, would give the song special meaning. Possibly without being able to articulate it, Ziegfeld may have sensed some of the compelling dichotomies that so singularly enriched and deepened her art. Not only was there the ability to move swiftly from rambunctious Jewish cut-up to universal mistress, there was much more. While many critics hailed her comedy as "wild" or "raucous," discerning critics such as Gilbert Seldes could also praise "the utmost economy of means" she employed to provoke laughter. Some have written that she was a skinny-legged, poorly-figured girl with a wide-mouthed, hooked-nosed face, while others recalled her figure as dignified and her face, except when she played with it for comic purposes, as warm and not unattractive.

But it was probably that mixture of humor and pathos that most accounted for her greatness. She returned often to skits and songs about ballet girls and ballet (which she pronounced "belly"), to her satiric vamps ("I may be a bad woman, but I'm awfully good company"), or her would-be overthrowers ("Rewolt! Rewolt!"), but beneath the hilarity lay years of artistic, sexual, and social pain.

Arguably Miss Brice's equal in comic skills but otherwise markedly different was one of her co-stars in the 1920 and 1921 editions, W. C. Fields. He had progressed light years from the juggler of just a few seasons back to a most highly developed comic style. There was nothing of pathos in his art, nor even of warmth. Portly, with grayish blond hair, vulpine eyes, a bulbous nose, and a reedy, croaky voice, his wit had become cerebral, impersonal, and waspish. Where Fanny Brice found smiling good humor in every figure she played, however much she tilted toward caricature, Fields played only himself, and that self reveled in insult and hypocrisy, mustering a wan smile only when it served his ends. Miss Brice in her comedy dealt with small, immediate situations; Fields was forever the boozy, churlish, cold Quixote battling such looming eternal bugaboos as honesty, legality, sobriety, and children. In Fields's skits, whether he was attempting to fix an automobile, take a nap, enjoy a picnic, or catch a train, he was beset by bratty youngsters, nagging wives, rude officials. To Miss Brice life was a challenge, to Fields, a personal conspiracy against him. Miss Brice's response to problems was essentially a laugh and a shrug, Fields's was a snarl, a sneer, a whine, or a verbal barb. However, like Miss Brice, and indeed probably like all great clowns, Fields basically developed only a small handful of character types and attitudes. Thus, in his last Broadway appearance, a 1930 book musical, *Ballyhoo*, Fields was still reaping the harvest he had planted in his first *Follies*. Just as in 1915 he had earned the name "Honest John" by returning the glass eye to its rightful owner, so fifteen years later he changed his mind about robbing a man after he learned the man was armed, walking away and muttering, "A thing like that wouldn't be honest."

Perhaps in remaining loyal to his greatest performers Ziegfeld unintentionally furthered the sense of sameness that began to erode the *Follies'* special aura. By 1923, and even more so in 1924, critics were lamenting something hand-me-down about the new editions. Tradition rather than vitality and imagination was propelling the series. Much of the 1925 edition consisted of salvage from a failed musical, *The Comic Supplement,* including its star, Fields, and some Norman Bel Geddes settings. In 1926, for the first time in twenty years, no *Follies* appeared in New York. The absence was caused in part by a legal battle. In the end, Ziegfeld rechristened a revue he had presented under several different titles during its tryout and New York run and toured it as the *Follies of 1926.* The road, always more conservative, was apparently delighted. But New York seems to have cared little. In 1927 Ziegfeld discarded his policy of star-filled *Follies* and based his whole edition on a single performer, Cantor. As they had in 1919, the producer and the singing-comedian fought, and once again Ziegfeld was forced to close a show when his star walked out. The edition had cost him $280,000 (two weeks after it opened, *Good News* was brought in for a more typical $75,000). When it closed, the era of the *Ziegfeld Follies* effectively came to an end. Shortly before his death Ziegfeld mounted one more *Follies.* The year was 1931, the country was in a great Depression, and all too many playgoers and critics perceived this edition, mounted for the first time at the Ziegfeld Theatre, as a sad echo from the past. Ziegfeld didn't help matters by reviving "Shine On, Harvest Moon" from the 1908 edition. A forced run kept the work alive for twenty weeks.

There would be later *Follies,* but not with Ziegfeld at the helm. The Shuberts produced most of them, but, regardless of who bankrolled the mountings and despite the success several enjoyed, the old magic was gone. Ziegfeld, like other great figures, had been the right man at the right time. If no one else had ever spent so much on productions, no one else had ever coupled expenditure with such unerring taste. He had brought to the *Follies* not only a singular, unrivaled beauty (and it is largely this for which he is remembered), but a pervasive sense of balance that had finally locked in place the bases for great revues. The often cantankerous, brahmin George Jean Nathan, no lover of musicals as a rule, once wrote of the great editions: "Out of the vulgar leg-show, Ziegfeld has fashioned a thing of grace and beauty, of loveliness and charm; he knows quality and mood. He has lifted, with sensitive skill, a thing that was mere food for smirking baldheads and downy college boys out of its low estate and into a thing of symmetry and bloom." Woollcott was right: Ziegfeld was that kind of producer, and there weren't many of them in this world.

4

Revolution/Evolution

Given the prolonged, post-Broadway tour of the 1907 *Follies*, it would appear that the edition was actually a bigger success than has been realized. But it might well have been merely one of many healthy single-season successes had not Ziegfeld persisted. By persisting with subsequent, increasingly adroit and memorable editions, the producer gave his *Follies* another sort of success, the kind that is enduring and legendary. But that sort of success is cumulative, coming only with time. In the first seasons after the 1907 *Follies* premiered and while Ziegfeld was nurturing and developing his art, other revues were few and far between—rarely more than one or two a season. The meager list includes *The Gay White Way* (1907), *The Merry-Go-Round* (1908), *The Mimic World* (1908), *The Merry Whirl* (1910), and *Up and Down Broadway* (1910). None were earth-shaking entertainments. Most were still "summer musicals," and all, except possibly *The Mimic World*, were still loosely plotted.

However, by early 1911, after four editions had appeared and a fifth was in the works, the *Follies* had gained both a unique momentum and national celebrity. Broadway's most notorious copycats, the Messrs. Shubert, watched enviously, well aware of the profits and renown that were eluding them. They decided to pounce, although their decision may have been motivated not only by their anxiety to deprive Ziegfeld (and his close allies and the Shuberts' principal rivals, Klaw and Erlanger) of some ticket sales and some fame, but also because they themselves had recently suffered some embarrassing failures in another field. That field was operetta, and while the brothers would later become closely identified with many major operetta successes their luck at this moment had run out.

Operetta, specifically Viennese operetta, had become the darling of Broadway ever since the opening of *The Merry Widow* in October of 1907, just short of four months after the premiere of the first *Follies*. From then until the outbreak of World War I, seven years later, operetta remained the reigning, most respected form of musical theater in America. Expecting the sui generis Hippodrome extravaganzas, Viennese operettas such as *The Merry Widow, The Chocolate Soldier, The Dollar Princess, A Waltz Dream, The Spring Maid*, and *Sari* and such American equivalents as *Naughty Marietta, The Pink Lady*, and *The Firefly* were regularly among the biggest hits of their season and won the highest critical praise for the excellence of their music and the solidity of their librettos. By contrast even the most successful musical comedies were generally seen to have inferior scores. Their biggest song hits were often interpolations and not written by the principal composer. And their main attraction was more often than not their star or stars. Their books remained loose and threadbare, thus creating in many playgoers and critics' minds an uncertainty, since revues, too, continued to offer slim, slapdash plots.

As we have noted a kindred spirit between operetta and the Ziegfeldian revue, it may be telling that Ziegfeld developed his form against this backround of operetta's vogue and that the Shuberts, who so dearly loved operetta, also became staunch promoters of the opulent, drapey revue. The comparison of operetta and revue should not be carried too far. After all, despite notable exceptions, particularly in the fashionable Viennese school, operetta waltzed primarily in exotic lands and distant times, while revue, like musical comedy, kept its eyes on and its rhythms and melodies attuned to contemporary America and, as often as not, contemporary New York. Yet musical comedy was far more consistent and persistent in this loyalty than was revue. If we recall the patriotic pageantry of some Ziegfeld numbers, the unabashed romantic settings of others—the medieval picture of a Ben Ali Haggin tableau and the quaint Dutch garden of "Tulip Time"—we see that the revues' affections clearly strayed with some regularity towards the worlds that were the domain of operetta. Even the extravagant, almost unreal costumes that were a stock in trade of Ziegfeldian revues trafficked in the appeal of the exotic that was far more akin to operetta than to musical comedy's flashily up-to-date, localized chauvinism. In a sense operetta and extravagant revue were always more escapist than musical comedy.

Be that as it may, when the Shuberts opened their great new flagship, the Winter Garden, on Broadway in 1911 they opened it with a revue, *La Belle Paree*. As far as theatrelovers are concerned, besides affording playgoers their first glimpse of a great new theatre, *La Belle Paree* is best recalled as the show in which Al Jolson made his sensational debut. But to students of revue the show is significant in that it demonstrates how unventuresome the producers were, for their show was yet another grab bag of skits and songs tied together by a time-worn tour-of-the-city plot, albeit in this instance 1911 Paris instead of New York. Moreover, the revue initiated an era in which the Shuberts were the most active advocates of revue. For a time, one revue after another followed *La Belle Paree* into the Winter Garden, prodigally expending the Shuberts' limited stock of ideas and talent while Ziegfeld concentrated on his annual *Follies*. The Shuberts themselves may have been aware of this and recognized that for all the success their revues achieved they were not seriously rivaling Ziegfeld. So during the next year one of the revues to tread the Winter Garden's boards was their initial offering in a series of projected annuals, *The Passing Show of 1912*. The show, which will be discussed in more detail in the next chapter, did begin a series that found a certain durability and measure of fame, but never seriously questioned Ziegfeld's supremacy as later annuals by other producers were to.

Slowly, perhaps almost imperceptibly at first, what was to be called "the deluge of revues" had begun. However, it took the outbreak of World War I to open fully the gates for the flood tide and also to bring on stage creative talents willing to change the very nature of the American musical revue.

Even before America's entry into the war, the bloody European battles had played havoc with the rage for operetta. After all, imported operettas were largely Austrian or German in origin, and many playgoers, alienated by the behavior of the Central Powers, were not willing to separate politics and art. By contrast, musical comedy had long been perceived as American or at least Anglo-American in origin and revue as totally American or at least Franco-American, so that both could appeal not only to native patriotism but to sympathy for the leading Allies.

The season of 1914–15 brought matters to a head, and altered forever the nature of American musical theatre—not merely American revue. At the very outset of the season Jerome Kern's "They Didn't Believe Me," interpolated into the imported English musical comedy, *The Girl from Utah*, propelled the 4/4 ballad into the forefront of theatre music, replacing the "alien" waltz as the principal style of theatre writing. Near the end of the season Kern joined with Guy Bolton to initiate the Princess Theatre musical comedies, a series, which P. G. Wodehouse later helped write, that established the mold for modern American musical comedy. In between these openings Irving Berlin wrote an entire score in ragtime—or at least what was perceived commercially as ragtime—for *Watch Your Step*. American settings, mannerisms, and ideas were quickly replacing European formulas.

On Christmas night of the same season George M. Cohan offered his own special gift to playgoers, the revue *Hello, Broadway!*. Years before Cohan himself had led the way in developing American musical comedy, but by 1914 his inspiration had seemingly waned, and it was largely felt that he was simply rehashing old themes and methods. The feeling was neither entirely fair nor accurate. Certainly, *Hello, Broadway!*, in its own way, was as much a landmark as his old musical comedies, even if it failed to leave behind the lasting melodic hits his older shows had. First of all, Cohan brought the revue into the relatively small Astor Theatre. At the same time he consciously discarded the sometimes deadeningly heavy opulence that had characterized the Ziegfeld and Shubert revues. This allowed Cohan to move the show at a pace heretofore unseen in revues (and Cohan had the reputation of speeding all his shows at breakneck tempos) and also, to a degree because of the theatre's size, effected a certain intimacy with the audience. Most importantly, however, Cohan made one addition, using a theatrical gimmick that became the talk of the season. At intervals throughout the evening one character or another carried a hat box on stage. The box supposedly contained the plot of the revue. At the end of the evening three of the characters met, and a brief dialogue ensued:

> McCluskey: Ah Ha! That hat box. Now to reveal the plot of the play. (Opens the box) Empty!
>
> Babbit: What became of the plot?
>
> George: There never was a plot.

Cohan had introduced the modern revue.

Indeed revues were to be a center of attention and conversation all season long. Leading newspapers, as well as trade sheets such as *Variety* and the *Dramatic Mirror,* ran major articles on them. Caught up in the excitement, the articles were not always careful in their distinctions. Probably playgoers were not, either. Thus, at one time or another, such shows as *Watch Your Step* and the Fred Stone–Dave Montgomery musical comedy extravaganza, *Chin-Chin,* were enveloped by the fervor and treated as revues. Certainly the well-plotted *Chin-Chin,* for all the extraneous nonsense Montgomery and Stone so deftly inserted, was not one. Whether *Watch Your Step* was is moot. Its programs contained the much-publicized by-line "Plot (if any) by Harry B. Smith" and Smith's hackneyed tour-of-the-town story was singularly shopworn and indifferent. Nonetheless, characterizations were reasonably maintained, and the variety of material was scarcely as slapdash as in most revues, so the show must probably go down in the books as musical comedy. The argument is academic in any case. What counts is that Broadway had become alive to the revue. Shortly before *Hello, Broadway!* opened, the *Dramatic Mirror,* in an article headed "More Revues Coming," observed, "The revue, which for the last two years has been the most popular form of musical entertainment in London and Paris, is invading New York with the force and dispatch of the German Army . . . The revue seems to be what the public wants . . ." Reacting to a similar observation of his own, Cohan, two weeks after *Hello, Broadway!*'s premiere, announced on the front page of *Variety* that he hoped "the permanent policy of the Astor Theatre in the future will be for 'revues'," and that his show's cast would serve as the nucleus for a stock company there. That hope was never realized. But thanks in no small part to Cohan and *Hello, Broadway!* the revue would move on in new directions.

That movement was anything but rash and, while all semblance of plots rapidly disappeared from the form, older traditions of grandeur and opulence continued to flourish. Indeed it was not until after World War I that a handful of new-style revues reinforced the evolution in the form.

One short-lived series, which actually premiered in the last full year of the war and which went through four editions from 1917 to 1920, was the brainchild of Raymond Hitchcock, whom Stanley Green has described as "a lanky, raspy-voiced comic with sharp features and straw-colored hair that he brushed across his forehead." His comedy was intimate, homespun, and filled with small-town slang. Critics were quick to observe that like Cohan he eschewed lavish spectacle, although in the first program he professed that wartime economies had forced the scaling down of sets and costumes. He claimed *Hitchy Koo, 1917* had set him back a mere $15,000. His later editions became a bit more elaborate, but his revues were as tasteful as they were pleasant and humorous. Nor were they devoid of melody. Out of the 1919 edition came Cole Porter's first hit, "Old Fashioned Garden." Jerome Kern wrote the score for the 1920 edition (although it was one of his lesser achievements), and Porter created the songs for a 1922 edition that folded during its tryout.

Another series is something of a curiosity, since it seemed designed to have the best of both worlds, the old and the new. It sprang from the inspiration of a young man who had worked as a ballroom dancer and a night-club master of ceremonies, and had begun to produce elegant little cabaret revues, mostly at the Palais Royal. His name was John Murray Anderson, and at first he called his new revue *Greenwich Village Nights*. By the time the show opened on July 15, 1919, at the bandbox Greenwich Village Theatre near Sheridan Square, its title had been changed to *Greenwich Village Follies*. The change goaded Ziegfeld to haul Anderson into court, where the older man soon learned to his dismay that he had no unique claim to the word "Follies."

The change in title was itself indicative of Anderson's ambivalence, since by 1919 the *Follies* had indisputably come to connote a special richly laden glamour. It was a glamour that Anderson obviously felt he could not ignore and on which he hoped to capitalize. To that end, although the small budget and tiny stage precluded elaborate decor, he filled the stage with what he himself called "colorful set pieces," adding "costumes were artful and 'arty,' down to the last gusset and seam." For most of its eight editions the imaginative beauty of these *Follies* made them the major rival of Ziegfeld's. Painter Reginald Marsh, Lady Duff Gordon (Lucille), James Reynolds, Erté, and Robert Locher were among Anderson's noted designers. Only the first two editions of the revue opened in the Village. These were quickly enlarged and moved to Broadway, where the remaining editions premiered. Many of New York's most perceptive critics rued the move. They recognized the high artistic quality of the productions at the same time they felt the other side of Anderson's coin—his intimacy, his rapport with his tiny, select audience, and his modern chic—was lost or tarnished in larger quarters.

Anderson's roster of performers, like Ziegfeld's, was a mixture of established stars and rising young talents. His list included Bessie McCoy Davis (famous in earlier times as "The Yama Yama Girl"), Ted Lewis, Bert Savoy (the "campy" drag queen) and his partner, Jay Brennan, Frank Crumit, Joe E. Brown, the Dolly Sisters, Blossom Seeley, Moran and Mack, and Benny Fields. His shows were never as jam-packed with stars as were Ziegfeld's, and even in retrospect few of his stars attained the stratosphere of celebrity that so many of Ziegfeld's did.

Although the *Greenwich Village Follies* left behind such memorable songs as "When My Baby Smiles at Me," "Three O'Clock in the Morning," and Cole Porter's "I'm in Love Again," the revues were not all that distinguished melodically. But in another area they did pioneer in moving the revue away from the written and spoken word toward an emphasis on music, or at least music and dance, for practically from the start Anderson incorporated one or more major ballet numbers. Beginning with the 1922 edition, with the balletic staging of Oscar Wilde's "The Nightingale and the Rose," Anderson offered a number of highly esteemed "ballet ballads." These dance numbers became a high point of the series, subtly tilting the emphasis of the shows.

Along with several subsequently initiated annuals, the *Greenwich Village Follies* at its most innovative broadcast a glimpse of the future. Yet, at heart, all these relatively long-lived series were straddlers, still trying to retain the best of both older and newer traditions. For the most part, it remained for individual revues, such as Cohan's *Hello, Broadway!* to prod the revue into genuine experimentation and change.

Perhaps some small note should be taken here of a revue which opened several months after the first appearance of the *Greenwich Village Follies*. The show was *Elsie Janis and Her Gang*, and it was little more than an inexpensive vaudeville, offering material with which its bantam star, the "Sweetheart of A.E.F.," and her associates had entertained troops during the recent war. The revue's run was short, although it toured the country off and on for several seasons and even returned briefly to New York three years later. Essentially it was what Baral has termed "the personality revue," a vehicle for a single star. The time was clearly not yet ripe for what a later generation would welcome as a one-man or one-woman show in which the star was alone on stage for virtually the entire evening, at best being relieved now and then by the smallest handful of performers while a costume was changed. Yet however unwittingly, Miss Janis was planting the seeds for this sort of evening. Certainly most critics had little time for her supporting cast, devoting the overwhelming bulk of their notices to the star.

Later in the 1920s a few other stars, most conspicuously Ed Wynn, would offer similar entertainments, albeit usually on a more elaborate, traditional scale. Wynn's first offering, *Ed Wynn's Carnival*, was forced on him after producers who bridled at his vocal militancy during the

Actors' Equity strike refused to hire him. Wynn was peculiar in many ways. In one sense he was the ideal revue star, for his attempts to sustain a character or help develop a story line in book shows always proved hopeless. Moreover, he worked best alone, responding only to a receptive audience and having them respond to him. And whereas most great comics achieved their laughs by being destructive—by puncturing a pretension, by cynical observation, or even by bald insult—Wynn won over playgoers by being lovable and by trafficking in a childlike innocence. Most critics agreed his material was usually awful and only Wynn could have made it seem wonderfully funny. His trademarks were his ludicrous costumes, his lisp, his fluttering hands and squeaky giggle, and his outlandish puns. In the *Carnival* he struggled in vain to return a book to some flats painted to resemble library shelves and later conversed with the audience while sitting on a prop fire. In his 1921 *The Perfect Fool* he offered his "non-eye-destroying spoon for iced tea," the spoon bending over the rim of the glass when the glass was raised, and he also did a mind-reading act dressed as a "rah-rah-rajah" who sucked lollipops. So personal, so one-to-one was Wynn's humor that after the final curtain he often dashed to the lobby to greet and joke with departing patrons. One critic noted, "When Wynn is absent the Carnival is just average revue," a truism for almost anything starring Wynn.

The important point was that these single-star shows, with their increasing, almost personal interaction between headliner and audience, were another tentative step away from the grandiose impersonality of the extravagant revues, and, more significantly, away from the artful generic balance that had been achieved.

Wynn's show, however, opened in April 1920, thus jumping a month head in our chronology. Curiously, it was John Murray Anderson who introduced some of the next advances, and not in his *Follies*. In March 1920, with the backing of the noted financier and philanthropist Otto Kahn, he produced *What's in a Name?* As Anderson observed,

> This revue had many innovations, which have been copied ever since. For the first time in a musical show drapes and draw curtains, of exquisite

material and design, replaced cumbersome painted scenery, wings and drops. The "treadmill," or moving stage platform, was introduced for the first time in America [he is wrong about that], and perhaps most significant of all, "projected scenery." In *What's In a Name?* there were great screens, thirty feet in height, on the panels of which scenes were projected by light.

Reynolds created both costumes and sets. That the advances were decorative rather than substantive was of little matter. They gave a new feeling to the revue and allowed for a faster pacing that was to be requisite in the speed conscious 1920s. Alexander Woollcott advised his readers that the production marked "the most beautiful staging . . . New York has known." In truth, performers and their material were probably not of the first quality, and the revue appears to have been little more than an artfully mounted vaudeville. Woollcott, noting that "It is really a Summer show which arrived with the sleet and snow—like an importunate crocus," concluded, "It is scant in its supply of humor, and musically it is ordinary." Of its songs, only "A Young Man's Fancy" enjoyed some small popularity outside the theatre. The number was staged against Reynolds's citron-yellow taffeta backdrop. Performers in eighteenth-century dress and looking like Dresden figurines (the pastel costumes for this number were by Locher) danced and sang around and even on top of a huge period music box. While the show was not presented in a tiny off-Broadway house, it did play the intimate Maxine Elliott's Theatre. But not for long. Perhaps because it offered no big names, little solid comedy, and no truly superior songs, the musical survived less than three months. Anderson was apparently so preoccupied with visual considerations, he neglected to supply a totally balanced, satisfying show.

That more satisfying revue came in 1922, and it came from Russia, by way of Paris. *Chauve-Souris* was the work of Russian émigrés, who had left their homeland after the Revolution and settled in France. Apart from a running commentary by its compère, the chubby, moon-faced Nikita Balieff, who introduced each of the numbers in his thickly accented, comically broken English, there was no spoken material. It was an evening of song and dance, including the show-stopping "Parade of the Wooden Soldiers." It had none of the heavyweight grandeur of the leading annuals, and it had its momentary lapses, but it also had a singular verve, color, and charm, so it racked up 544 performances—the longest run of any revue up to its time—then toured the country and returned at intervals to New York all during the 1920s.

By contrast, *The 49ers*, which opened at the end of the same year, lasted a mere two weeks. Yet on paper the revue promised to be as dazzlingly successful as *Chauve-Souris* had been. The awesome list of credits featured the brightest lights of the Algonquin's celebrated Round Table and thus became a roster of America's leading wits: Franklin P. Adams, Robert Benchley, Heywood Broun, Marc Connelly, George S. Kaufman, Ring Lardner, Dorothy Parker, and Robert E. Sherwood. Only in their determination to discard spectacle and avoid haphazard vaudeville did their approach at all touch that of the Russians. But whereas the Russian answer was basically musical, the American answer was verbal. To read the happier critical notices is to believe they succeeded wildly and that the merriment was unceasing. Among the skits which especially delighted critics were Benchley and Parker's "Nero," a spoof of overwrought historical dramas in which, with a cavalier disdain for chronological integrity, Robespierre, Queen Victoria, Generals Grant and Lee, and Benito Mussolini had a brief, uncomfortable encounter; Broun's Pirandelloish retelling of Hans Christian Andersen's "The King's New Suit of Clothes"; Connelly's "Chapters from 'American Economics,' " which consisted of two dances: "The Autumn Dance of Hat-Check Girls," celebrating the seasonal upturn in trade, and "The Spring Dance of Small-Town Mayors," rejoicing in the spurt in retail business occasioned by the switch from winter to warm-weather underwear; Ring Lardner's nonsense piece, "The Tridget of Greva"; Kaufman's "Life in the Back Pages," in which middle-class American conversations are seen to consist entirely of advertising slogans; and Adams's "The Love Girl," demonstrating how Graustarkian operetta of the Romberg and Friml school could be wedded to modern business notions. No one seemed to notice or care about the music which Lewis Gensler provided whenever some was required.

Burns Mantle perceptively hailed the show as "a new form of revue," and welcomed its steadfast cleverness, while the *Times*'s often dyspeptic Corbin commented, "The prevailing tone is of the best contemporary wit and tom foolery," and predicted a long run. Yet, looking back forty-five years later, Connelly still recalled "the chill of its first-night reception" and remembered *Vanity Fair*'s savvy editor, Frank Crowninshield, remarking to him, "Maybe I missed the point, but was it all supposed to take place in an insane asylum?"

Granted that the material had its inevitable ups and downs, the best of it still reads hilariously. So why, then, the strangely mixed reaction, and why the dismal failure? Of course, in 1922 the great names attached to the show had not all built their reputations to the heights they would enjoy in later years. Moreover, competition was fierce. Within a week of *The 49ers* premiere, *Rain* (the season's most sensational hit), George M. Cohan's *Little Nellie Kelly*, and Kaufman and Connelly's own *Merton of the Movies* had opened and lured playgoers to line up at box offices. But that was nothing unusual at the time. The theatre was far healthier and far more active than in later days. Even divided notices often failed to discourage theatregoers, and *The 49ers* was housed in a minuscule theatre that didn't need many sales to sell out.

Certainly one explanation—though it naturally fails to provide a total answer—is that while the revue moved in a new direction, it was the wrong direction. Audiences delighted in musical shows because they were musical and showy. *The 49ers* was neither. It was essentially literary, and, by theatrical extension, verbal. Quite possibly much of the material that still reads so humorously did not play as well—or was not played as well. But more to the point, settings and melody were relegated to the background. Even the most avant-garde theatregoers who were crying for more intimacy, more artful stylishness, and more stepped-up pacing apparently really wanted these advances within traditional forms. An evening devoted almost entirely to skits was too intellectually demanding, denying the comfortable, attractive, well-balanced escapism of revues which also offered beautiful sets and costumes, and seductive melodies. Thus, all unknowingly, the failure of *The 49ers* turned a spotlight on the future of American musical revue, which would end often simply as a review of music.

Whatever the individual failings of these earlier revues as they attempted to move the form into modern times, a revue that arrived in 1924 was seen by contemporaries to have virtually everything and by many historians as the show that truly sounded the death knell for the more mammoth older-style extravaganza. Playbills and advertisements seemed a trifle uncertain about its title, calling it at one time or another by such variations as *André Charlot's Revue*, *Charlot's London Revue*, and *The Charlot Revue of 1924*, this last title suggesting that it might become another annual. Most playgoers called it simply *Charlot's Revue*. It was as chock full of significance for the American musical theatre as it was of balanced entertainment for 1924 audiences.

Perhaps the least obvious facet of its significance is that it was English. The importance of the English to our musical theatre is too often neglected. Our first musical entertainments were English ballad operas, which were sometimes imitated to provide the first native musical plays. Then English opera briefly became the rage. But it was the arrival of *H.M.S. Pinafore* in 1879, the "Pinafore craze" it initiated, and the subsequent success and example of other Savoyard comic operas that truly opened all our stages to musical theatre and prodded the first major American librettists and composers to attempt American models. Similarly, the Gaiety musical comedies which started to arrive here in the mid-1890s furthered the development of our own musical comedies by their cohesiveness and style. (A decade or so later the English launched into the making of extensive original-cast recordings, but we were shamefully laggard in following their lead.) Now once more, this time with a single revue, the English again pushed us into a new era.

Of course, in one small respect *Charlot's Revue* was not totally English, since Charlot, as his name suggests, was a Frenchman. He was born in Paris in 1882 and while still a young man served in various capacities—press agent, business manager, and manager—of a number of Paris playhouses and music halls. He was thirty years old when he took over the faltering Alhambra on London's Leicester Square and with M. V. Leveaux produced an elaborate revue called *Kill That Fly!* However, he did not hit full stride until four years later when he took over the Vaudeville Theatre on the Strand and began mounting more intimate revues with simple, seemingly inane titles such as *Some, Cheep, Tabs,* and *Buzz-Buzz.* By the time he decided to brave New York he had some thirty revues under his belt. And, indeed, the show New York so swiftly took to its heart would not have seemed so very novel to West End playgoers, for not only had they long since become familiar with this sort of revue but the material he brought with him had been culled from his past successes' best moments. Moreover, he brought many of his favorite performers along. Much of the material was from the pen of a then unknown Noel Coward, while the equally unheard of players included Jack Buchanan, Gertrude Lawrence, and Beatrice Lillie.

Aging playgoers with long memories still recall fondly several of the revue's high points. They remember Miss Lillie's helter-skelter madness as she created mayhem while exhorting a band of Amazons to "March with Me," and Gertrude Lawrence singing Coward's 'Parisian Pierrot" and the hit of the show, "Limehouse Blues." In short, they recall the musical high points. Largely forgotten are the non-musical comic sketches, although critics reported many of them were first-rate. And while several reviewers, although praising the sets and costumes, complained that they were below the best American standards, some oldtimers can still describe the clown's costume Miss Lawrence wore and the beribboned guitar she carried in the Pierrot number. Comedy was not unappreciated, but songs and beauty carried the day. Thus, besides furthering the importance of the English stage to the American musical theatre and introducing several names which would rise to luminous heights on our stages, *Charlot's Revue* caught precisely the very balanced advances sophisticated audiences were looking for in the genre.

As we have always done, however, Americans soon enough showed that we could match or even beat the British at the game. We showed it first of all in the earliest of the masterful American new wave revues, *The Garrick Gaieties.* The history of this short-lived series is interesting. In 1925 the Theatre Guild had built its own playhouse on West 52nd Street, but had run out of ready cash to finish decorating the building. So the company mounted a tastefully put together revue on a shoestring, trusting that the income from a handful of special performances would give it the additional monies it required. The first-night reception was such that the revue was brought back for a run, much of which it played at the Guild it had helped beautify.

No small part of the revue, falling back on a tradition as old as the first *Passing Show*, was concerned with twitting hit Broadway plays, although since so many Broadway hits of the day were produced by the Guild, the humor was often deliciously self-deprecating. For example, the Guild's much acclaimed mounting of Sidney Howard's *They Knew What They Wanted* was reincarnated as "They Didn't Know What They Were Getting." But while intra-theatrical matters dominated the evening, time was found to poke fun at such obvious targets as Calvin Coolidge (up past his bedtime), the Scopes "Monkey Trial" (with jurors in monkey suits), New York's corrupt police, the three musketeers, and New Yorkers' subway manners. The most beautiful production number was played out against a multicolored set by the well-known artist Miguel Covarrubias and featured a dance by his wife, Rose Rolando. But from the opening number, "Gilding the Guild," with its brilliantly witty rhymes and infectious melody the songs told delighted playgoers that even something better was afoot. The songs were the work of a pair of relative newcomers, Richard Rodgers and Lorenz Hart, and included two that would be among their standards, "Manhattan" and "Sentimental Me." A year later a second edition introduced "Mountain Greenery." A third and final edition, without Rodgers and Hart, appeared in 1930.

However, for the 1926 edition Rodgers and Hart created one of American revue's masterful little gems, a spoof of operetta called "Rose of Arizona." That Rodgers, with his penchant for operetta-like waltzes and his eventual drift into operetta when he joined with Oscar Hammerstein II, was co-author is interesting, especially since the sort of operetta satirized was not the traditional Graustarkian variety, set in distant or imaginary royal kingdoms, but American operetta with the hero often a member of or closely allied to some American policing force—operettas such as *Naughty Marietta* and *Rose-Marie*. The heroine of the parody, Gloria, loves Capt. Allan Sterling, police chief of Rose Raisa, Arizona. Gloria is kidnapped by the bandit Caramba, so

Sterling must rescue her before they can wed. If, like the later, full-length *Little Mary Sunshine*, the playlet was not particularly scrupulous about aiming its barbs, often shooting at targets in other fields, it was capital fun. An amusing footnote is that when Ziegfeld presented the operetta *Rio Rita* a year later, it bore some striking, albeit no doubt unintentional resemblances to the parody. Thus, while Capt. Sterling and his men sing of the "Hootin', scootin' land of Arizona," *Rita's* Capt. Stewart and his Texas Rangers exclaimed they were "rootin' pals, hootin' pals, scootin' pals, shootin' pals."

Brief mention ought to be made here of one other fondly remembered series, *The Grand Street Follies*. Six editions were presented, one each succeeding year beginning in 1924. These originally bantam revues were mounted at first in Greenwich Village by a local theatre group at the end of its regular seasons, and were devoted almost exclusively to parodying their own productions and Broadway successes. Travesties brandished such titles as "What Price Morning-Glories" (really not half so funny as a contemporary collegiate show which was called *Glory! What Prices!*) and "They Knew What They Wanted Under the Elms." The laughter was in the hands of a small band of mightily skilled comics, especially the superb mimic Albert Carroll, and the deft comedienne Dorothy Sands. Music was undistinguished when it was not derivative; scenery and costumes were minimal. Like the *Greenwich Village Follies*, the show made the mistake of finally moving uptown, where so much of the charm and bite was lost that, with the coming of the Depression, the series faded away.

Revues of all sizes and shapes flourished during the 1920s. Those examined in this chapter stand out not necessarily because they were the major hits of the time—and some, as we have seen, were quick failures—but rather because of their historical and aesthetic importance. Other revues of the era sometimes incorporated the advances these shows employed, but as a rule they did so without a similar consistency or brilliancy. Yet noteworthy or not the effect was telling on audiences of the period, who came to see in these revues the latest word in entertainment and who simultaneously came to view the great annuals as obsolescent. Apart from his random revival of 1931, Ziegfeld for all practical purposes closed the book on his *Follies* with the 1927 edition. *The Greenwich Village Follies*, after a gap of several years, closed shop with its 1928 edition. The Shuberts' *Passing Shows*, which we will come to in more detail shortly, had thrown in the towel after 1924. Those annuals which managed to linger on a while longer were those which attempted to respond to the newer wave of revues, or in one case took a slightly different tack. However, they should not be ignored, so let's backtrack a bit and look at these great rivals to Ziegfeld.

5

Ziegfeld's Rivals:
The Other Great Annuals

The Shuberts were the busiest producers and most expansive theatre-owners in Broadway history. Between 1900 and 1945 they produced over five hundred plays on Broadway and at their height owned thirty-one New York playhouses and over sixty in other cities. Although their theatrical acumen was generally unquestioned, their reputation had its occasional ups and frequent downs. They were as feared and hated as they were respected.

Sam, Lee, and J. J. Shubert were born in Shervient, Lithuania, in the 1870s—the exact dates are a matter of dispute. They were brought to America in 1882 by their father, a ne'er-do-well alcoholic peddler, and settled in Syracuse, N.Y., where they discarded their original family name of Szemanski. A few years later Lee and Sam took odd jobs at local theatres, Sam soon rising to the post of treasurer at one of the houses. In 1894 Sam bought the area touring rights to Charles Hoyt's *A Texas Steer*, and before long the brothers were producing as well as running some small local playhouses. In 1900 they decided to tackle New York. It was a decision made in the face of the stranglehold held over all major American theatres at the time by nefarious Theatrical Trust and its hard-bitten boss, Abe Erlanger. Their dealings were brazen, byzantine, and usually successful. Within a short time they were regarded as the great hope for the theatre, the only men capable of destroying the Trust. Indeed, they smashed its seemingly impregnable monopoly with stunning rapidity. But their advocates soon realized that the brothers, now including young J.J. but no longer Sam, who had been killed in a 1905 train wreck, were as greedy and monopolistic as Erlanger. They made and broke contracts with a dismaying indifference. They had little or no loyalty. And their answer to a rival's success was to buy out the rival or, failing that, produce a copycat version of the success. It was this last practice which gave birth to *The Passing Shows*.

Ziegfeld at the time, and for most of his career, was closely allied with Erlanger, who had bankrolled the 1907 edition of the *Follies*. When the Shuberts realized that the *Follies* were on their way to becoming an institution and that they could not lure Ziegfeld into their camp, they concluded they had no choice but to set up a competitive series. Ziegfeld's success was a particular sore point to J.J., who was more volatile and emotional than Lee. It is generally perceived that he persuaded Lee to let him proceed with the revue. In a small way this is telling, since it was also J.J. who was the great lover and promoter of the operettas the brothers would produce.

Precisely how or why they came to choose the title is uncertain. The original *Passing Show* was relatively recent history—only eighteen years past—when they embarked on their series. By adopting the name the brothers may have felt they gave their shows a certain pedigree, a paid-for extension into history that reached further back than even the *Follies*. Moreover, by 1912 the Shuberts owned the Casino, where the show had been mounted, although they had no intention of presenting their revues at the house. They may have even seen it as a slap at Erlanger, since George Lederer, who had produced the 1894 revue, was still active and loyal to Erlanger, but, of course, had no legal way of protecting his old title. Whatever the brothers' reasoning, the title choice was the initial step in establishing the hand-me-down nature of their venture.

Their first edition was the second step. *The Passing Show of 1912*, presented as the latter and major half of a double bill, opened with passengers debarking from a newly arrived steamship. If that had a familiar ring to regular first-nighters, it was because they had watched a similar scene at the start of the 1911 *Follies* some months earlier. What followed was another tour-of-the-town, with a heavy emphasis on spoofing the theatrical hits of the moment. Interestingly, the work that preceded the revue was *The Ballet of 1830*, a three-scene mime-drama imported from London's Alhambra. It may have been added to bring a small touch of "class" to the whole evening, but it also, however unintentionally, foreshadowed the importance dance and music would have for much later revues.

As far as injecting an artistic note into the program, the Shuberts need not have been too concerned. They were shrewd and knowing showmen, so by contemporary standards their initial edition was itself rattling good theatre. Their roster of performers was almost the equal of that Ziegfeld was offering at the time, including as it did such rising young players as Willie and Eugene Howard, Charlotte Greenwood, Anna Wheaton, Oscar Schwarz (who as Oscar Shaw would soon be a popular leading man), Harry Fox, Jobyna Howland, and the somewhat older Trixie Friganza. To compose the basic score they called on their house composer, Louis Hirsch, a better melodist than any Ziegfeld had yet employed and who, but for his relatively early death, might have risen to greater heights. An added bonus was an interpolation by Irving Berlin, "The Ragtime Jockey Man," which Willie Howard turned into a show-stopper. Yet for all its worth as solid entertainment, the show lacked that seemingly incomparable touch which Ziegfeld brought to his shows, even in pre-Urban days. Among the critics there was virtually none of the breathless wonder that Ziegfeld's most imaginative moments had induced from the start. The production was clearly eye-catching and colorful, probably even a bit gaudy, but never ravishingly beautiful. Their attempt to give the evening some artistic respectability by tacking on the ballet suggests the Shuberts recognized this, but they were rarely able to command the consummate taste that Ziegfeld had on his own and which he elicited from others.

In all there were a dozen editions of *The Passing Show* between 1912 and 1924. Only 1920 was skipped, although the 1921 edition actually opened late in 1920. Years later the Shuberts attempted two more revivals, one in 1932, the other in 1945. Both folded out of town. But in their heyday, though they regularly took a back seat to Ziegfeld and sometimes to other revues, *The Passing Shows* were not without interest.

Two editions were especially noteworthy. Of the 1914 production, theatrical historian Cecil Smith has written, "The third *Passing Show* went down in history primarily as the moment of final triumph for the slender, modern chorus girl. Gone forever were the gigantic chorus ladies with their Amazonian marches and drills . . . girls' legs, which had been emerging from their tights inch by inch for several seasons, were now presented unadorned and *au naturel* . . . Skirts were short and arms were bare, and at one point the glittering spangles were dispensed with, revealing bare midriffs on the upper-class New York stage for the first time. The 'winsome witches' gave a new and piquant meaning to the runway."

Other scholars have generally concurred with Smith's assessment, although at this far remove it is difficult to be sure that any such gradual evolution did, in fact, have a "moment of final triumph." Ziegfeld's beauties had been growing slimmer from the beginning, responding to the new ideals of feminine beauty promoted in no small part by films. Moreover, the runway, while it brought the girls closer to patrons in front-row seats, was not the first attempt at a new intimacy. Ziegfeld had on several occasions paraded girls down the aisles. Nevertheless, thanks in large measure to Smith this perception persists, and there is no compelling reason to dispute it.

Contemporary critics, not having Smith's vantage point of history, viewed the edition differently, seeing not its historic significance but its immediate worth as entertainment. They were virtually unanimous in singling out three spectacular numbers as the highlights of the production. The *Herald* described the "Sloping Path" as "four paths built almost vertically from the floor of the stage to the top of the proscenium and along which sixty girls in white danced and ran." The *Sun* went

into even greater detail to depict the other two numbers, guessing cor-
rectly the mechanism behind "The Transatlantic Flight":

> Diving and rising like a huge bird, an airship rides over the water,
> and in its lighted interior one sees three of the characters of the play.
> It is the effect of the realistic water which is after all the most striking
> detail of the scene; and marvelously like nature the seething and foaming
> waves are. Possibly it is produced by some use of the cinematograph.

And then there was the scene depicting the burning of San Francisco,
which began, anachronistically, with tangoing couples routed from a
tea dance at the Palace Hotel by the onset of the earthquake and fire.

> The black frames of the burned buildings were still red from the
> flames that crept and licked up their black skeletons while clouds of
> smoke puffed and whirled into the heavens. The orchestra under Oscar
> Radin played the Feuerzauber from "The Walkuere" and the spectators
> decided that no more realistic illusion of fire could have been created.

The critic only later added that the scene ended with the transformation
of the ruins into the new Panama-Pacific Exposition just opening in
San Francisco. Having expended so many paragraphs on the eye-pop-
pers, reviewers could accord only terse, sometimes perfunctory praise
to a lengthy roster of performers, which included singer José Collins,
the hefty female impersonator George W. Monroe, and the beautiful,
versatile Marilyn Miller.

The very next year, 1915, *The Passing Show* gave promise of finally
rivaling the *Follies* in beauty and splendor. It garnered huge applause
for more sumptuous settings depicting the San Francisco Fair and also
Hawaii, but most of all for a lavish "Spring Ballet," which provided
the first-act finale and which featured the dancing of Miss Miller. Yet
reading between the lines of praise for the new edition it is clear the
hand-clapping was for Shubert showmanship and not Ziegfeld artistry.
Thus, the *Herald* insisted, "The new production is brightest and happiest
when it is the Winter Garden and naught else," while the *Sun* was
grateful for "the privilege of laughing at more spontaneous fun than

any recent Winter Garden piece has offered, of viewing the youngest and most attractive collection of young women of the chorus that this theatre has ever shown." Ziegfeld's answer was to hire away Miss Miller and bring Joseph Urban onto the scene, thus leaving behind permanently the Shuberts and their annuals.

The array of singers, dancers, and comedians which the Shuberts employed in the series remains impressive, although most were then either relative unknowns, such as Miss Miller, Charles King, Ed Wynn, Fred Allen, and Fred and Adele Astaire, or such fading older stars as Bessie Clayton, DeWolf Hopper, and Jefferson DeAngelis. The Howard Brothers appeared in the most editions, while other then popular performers included José Collins, James Barton, and George Jessel.

When Hirsch left the Shubert fold, Sigmund Romberg took his place and composed the principal scores for many of the productions. But the music Romberg wrote for these revues was more contemporary and more in an American idiom than the Austro-Hungarian style melodies that later made him famous. For all their gifts neither Hirsch nor Romberg, nor any of the other men who composed the revues' basic scores, created anything lasting. Enduring hits from *The Passing Shows* were all interpolations: "Pretty Baby" (1916), "Goodbye Broadway, Hello France!" (1917), "Smiles" and "I'm Forever Blowing Bubbles" (1918), and "Carolina in the Morning" (1922). By way of a historical footnote, the first George Gershwin melody introduced on Broadway, "Making of a Girl," was sung in the 1916 edition.

In the next major annual music loomed much larger—not just memorably melodic music, but often infectiously danceable music. What contemporaries tagged "the dancing craze" had exploded across America just before World War I with the return from Europe of Irene and Vernon Castle. At first the most popular dances were quite elegant, sedate affairs: the maxixe, the tango, the one-step, and the two-step. Within a very short time, however, dances became more gimmicky and utilized more picturesque names, such as the turkey trot and the grizzly bear. With the gimmickry came increasingly frenetic stepping. So it was not all that untoward that *George White's Scandals* should spring forth from the mind and artistry of a dancer. White was born George

Weitz in New York City in 1890. To help earn money for his family he served as a messenger and danced in streets and lesser Bowery theatres for the coins patrons threw to him. Apparently his family, however needy, objected to his dancing, so he ran away from home, serving for a brief time as a jockey, but mostly seeking jobs in vaudeville. He first performed for Broadway audiences when he earned applause and critical attention by dancing a clog in Deems Taylor's 1910 musical, *The Echo*. Increasingly prominent stints followed in two *Ziegfeld Follies* as well as several other producers' revues and musical comedies.

The first edition of the *Scandals*, in 1919, baffled many critics, already uncertain whether another annual was needed and whether White in any case was the man to bring it off. The revue prompted Burns Mantle's oft-quoted barb that "a hoofer should stick to his dancing." But, though a small postwar recession was settling in, theatrical economics were still sturdy enough to allow White to realize a sizable profit and give him time to think about improvements for his next edition. That second, 1920 edition was the turning point for the series, clarifying the approach that White would take and develop from there on. First of all, he recognized the importance of visually beautiful spectacle. Critics were to note that at their best the *Scandals* had eye-appeal comparable to that of the *Ziegfeld Follies*. Yet there were important distinctions. White's casts, and particularly his line of lovely girls, were smaller than Ziegfeld's, and the more elaborate scenes rarely seemed as sumptuously weighted down. This may have been in part the result of White's awareness that lightness and speed went hand in hand, for White brought his hoofer's love of fast pacing to all his shows. Just possibly, too, White may have seen the *Greenwich Village Follies* and accepted Anderson's startling simplicity and cleanness of line as the only road to the future. White also pioneered by injecting modern color schemes and textures into his spectacle. He leaned far less heavily on gaudiness than did the Shuberts or on soft pastels bathed in romantic lights than did Ziegfeld or Anderson. Instead he turned to more strikingly novel juxtapositions of colors and played far more than any other producer with blacks, grays, and whites. He was equally daring in his employment of leather, synthetics, and metallics for both sets and costumes. The effect seems to have been to have removed much of the *Scandals* from the inherently nostalgic, other-worldly realms suggested by then competing annuals and to have planted them squarely in the driving, harder machine age. The broad comedy of the sketches tilted in the same direction. While many *Scandals* skits still spoofed Broadway shows and other topics long the stock-in-trade of revue fun, a noticeably large proportion of them turned for laughs to modern political corruptino or changing social mores such as the increase in divorce, Prohibition, and Chicago gangsters. The difference was probably one of degree not kind, yet it helped give the *Scandals* their steely, cynical, sixty-mile-an-hour jazz-age tone.

But that jazz-age tone was nowhere better exemplified than in the dancing and the music that were the real attractions of the series. From the start virtually to the end White's shows were dancing shows. They were, as one critic wrote of the 1922 edition, "first and last, a dancer's idea of entertainment." White himself danced in them as did his long-time friend, tiny, dimple-kneed Ann Pennington. Tom Patricola, comic stepper Lester Allen, and a host of other lesser lights clogged, shimmied, tapped, and Charlestoned throughout the series. Eleanor Powell won applause in 1931; Ann Miller in 1939.

And what music they often danced to! No other revue series produced as long a list of durable standards as did this one. Moreover, the music was totally of a type and period, joyously reflecting the hedonistic excitement of the era of wonderful nonsense as well as its more pensive, bluesy moments. The songs for the first edition, primarily by Richard A. Whiting, Arthur Jackson, and White, gave no real indication of the melodious outpouring just around the corner. With the second edition White signed on young George Gershwin, who was to create the music for five successive productions and whose contributions included "I'll Build a Stairway to Paradise" (1922) and "Somebody Loves Me" (1924). In 1922 Gershwin and White attempted a twenty-five-minute jazz opera, "Blue Monday Blues," but it was too stark and too advanced for playgoers' tastes and was withdrawn after opening night. When Gershwin and White disagreed on financial matters, White replaced the composer with the team of DeSylva, Brown, and Henderson, who provided the scores for three editions. Earlier he had also enlisted the popular conductor, Paul Whiteman, to lead an onstage band. The new team's work on the 1926 presentation ranks with that of *The Band Wagon* and *This Is the Army* as one of the greatest of all revue scores, as we'll see shortly. In 1931, after DeSylva had left for Hollywood, Brown and Henderson wrote another collection of hits for that year's offering, headed by "Life Is Just a Bowl of Cherries," and including "My Song," "This Is the Missus," and "The Thrill Is Gone."

With songs like these of course White saw to it that his casts contained top-flight singers as well as dancers. Winnie Lightner and Frances Williams each graced three productions, while Harry Richman and Rudy Vallee appeared in two. Ethel Merman joined the 1931 show. Nor were comics overlooked, with the Howard Brothers, moving over from the *Passing Shows*, cavorting for six years and Lou Holtz for three.

Like Ziegfeld, White had not initially attached his name to his revues. He did that first in 1921. His series flourished just as the oldest annuals were giving up or fading away. By common consensus the high-water mark was reached with the 1926 edition.

The opening number proclaimed "Talent Is What the Public Wants," and the show went on to prove it was what the public got, although some playgoers were outraged at the $55 top for first-night tickets and a new *Scandals* high of $5.50 for orchestra seats subsequently. The comic moments, some musical, some not, flung poisonous darts at the latest excesses and absurdities. The Howard Brothers, whose skits were introduced by seven-year-old twins, the Hasting Sisters, lost a run-in with a lady barber and took a jaundiced look at their *Passing Show* days. They joined with Richman and Patricola to twit Park Avenue canines and their paid escorts in "Walking Dogs Around." Willie Howard also clowned as a husband trying to talk on the phone to his mistress while his wife was in the room; as commanding general in a Hatfield-McCoy-like feud; and as an inarticulate, partially nude hero of very modern drama (this in 1926!). Otto Kahn and J. P. Morgan's sitting down to examine the financial scene was a viable subject for satire, while the humorous song "David and Lenore" got its laughs at the expense of producer David Belasco and his reigning star of the moment, Lenore

Ulric. One sketch felt by some to be too venomous and to exceed the bounds of good taste was "A Western Union," which looked at the recent marriage of Irving Berlin to Ellen Mackay, whose dismayed father owned extensive telegraph interests.

Frances Williams and Richman sang the show's only really romantic number, a wistful ballad "The Girl Is You and the Boy Is Me." Spectacle was offered in "Sevilla," in which the singer who initially introduced the song was suddenly lifted up and out of sight to leave a bullring free for the dancers in bright Spanish costumes, and in "Lady Fair," which culminated with a "Triumph of Women" tableau presenting such historical stalwarts as Cleopatra, Lucretia Borgia, and Mme. DuBarry.

Three other numbers provided the evening's high points. Richman, complete with tuxedo, straw hat, cane, and lisp, announced this was his "Lucky Day." The chorus joined the celebration, while the comeliest of the mannequins paraded in costumes representing a wishbone, a horseshoe, a four-leaf clover, and other charms. According to the *American* the song was employed as a leitmotif throughout the evening. Ann Pennington, as cute and tiny as a button, stopped the show cold with "A new twister," "Black Bottom." She swung into the dance "like a baby bacchante, big eyes agleam, wide shoulders shaking, slim legs flying." John Anderson of the *Post* characterized the dance as a "slap-foot, drag-foot, cozy sort of dance" filled with "sinuous gyrations." It quickly established itself as second only to "The Charleston" in flapper popularity. White saved the show's biggest hit for a spot of special honor, the first-act finale, and gave it a curiously cluttered, drapey production, more like something out of Ziegfeld than his own more modern, steely spectacles. But it worked. "The Birth of the Blues" was presented as a battle between modern and classical music. White made no secret of which side he was on, since with an eye toward the patently preposterous he enlisted Willie Howard to represent Beethoven and brother Eugene to impersonate Liszt. By contrast the much prettier McCarthy Twins portrayed "St. Louis Blues" and "Memphis Blues." Perhaps in an attempt to redress the imbalance he brought out the even lovlier Fairbanks Twins to stand in for the music of Schubert and Schumann. (All the girls in this scene were gowned dazzlingly by Erté.) Richman sang the song and Miss Pennington danced briefly to it. As if to demonstrate that older and newer traditions could be accommodated at the same time, Gershwin's "Rhapsody in Blue" was performed (with special lyrics). In the end the company climbed a heavenly staircase flanked by gorgeous angels, angels and mortals alike all bathed in appropriately blue lights. A very anti-climactic second-act finale had the assembled cast ask the audience the musical question "Are You Satisfied?" By that time the answer must have been obvious.

The show ran over a year, nearly doubling the longest stand of any other *Scandals*. Partly because it ran so long, no 1927 edition appeared—the first break in the series. The next break occurred in 1930 when White was beset by financial problems, and film musicals, including some attempts at revues, were stealing Broadway's thunder as well as much of its talent. The excellent 1931 version, besides its fine cast and memorable songs, offered settings by Urban and costumes by Charles LeMaire, both of whom had been in Ziegfeld's camp until he abandoned his revues. But changing times and changing tastes were too much for White. His 1935 edition was sparingly budgeted, produced nothing memorable, and survived a forced run of fourteen weeks. The last version, billed as *George White's Scandals of 1939–40*, was seen by many as a hollow echo of past glories, although it left behind one final song hit, "Are You Havin' Any Fun?"

If the *Ziegfeld Follies* reflected the elegance, spaciousness, prodigality, and more leisurely attitudes of a pre-World War I society, certainly the *Scandals* captured the fundamental flavor and texture of the roaring twenties. In their jazz-colored music, their raucous comedy and high-kicking dances, in their frequent move away from the soft materials and hues of the past for their settings and costumes they mirrored the essence of a happy, carefree, and careless age.

Although the *Music Box Revues* survived for only four editions and though in none of them was anything startlingly daring or of an evolutionary nature attempted, yet their quality was such that they were recognized as forty-carat flawless gems of the revue form and are remembered with an affection denied several of the longer-lasting series. For the time being at least they have left behind the most solid monument to their more ephemeral magic—the exquisite little Music Box Theatre, which was built to house the revues.

Behind both the series and the playhouse stood two old friends—both tiny men themselves but both giants in their fields—producer Sam H. Harris and songwriter Irving Berlin. Harris had only recently dissolved a long-standing partnership with another little giant, George M. Cohan, while Berlin had apparently joined a growing list of figures who had quarreled with Ziegfeld, for whom he had provided basic scores for several *Follies*. (Berlin and Ziegfeld would be reunited for another *Follies* after the demise of the *Music Box Revues*.) Berlin, who was born Israel Baline in Russia in 1888, was brought to America while still a youngster. Raised on the Lower East Side, he helped support himself and his family by taking a job as a singing waiter. His first song, "Marie from Sunny Italy," was published in 1907. Fame came in 1911 with "Alexander's Ragtime Band." He had contributed to Broadway since 1910, although his first full score was not heard until *Watch Your Step* in 1914. While some commentators have remarked on the deceptive simplicity of his songs, he really had no instantly identifiable style. Rather, almost chameleon-like, he brilliantly adapted his style to the musical vogues of the moment.

Neither Harris nor Berlin was young, and while both were astute showmen with a clear understanding of tides in theatrical fashion, both also seemed to have strong emotional ties to an older manner of theatre, essentially the style that Ziegfeld had developed with such personal flair. As a result, despite some fine tuning for modern tastes, the *Music Box Revues* were to represent a step backward from the more advanced revues of the period. But they were to be done with such consummate skill that, at least at first, few objected and even many among the increasing number of critics who were finding revues repetitive and boring were willing to set aside their predilections.

The playhouse that Harris and Berlin built was an intimate one, far smaller than the theatres where the *Ziegfeld Follies*, *The Passing Shows*, or even the *Scandals* were presented. This was a knowing concession to more modern ideas, although in the end, for economic reasons, it hastened the disappearance of the series. The show on stage was another matter. The first edition, *The Music Box Revue of* 1921–22 (the series, except at the very start, regularly used theatre seasons as designations instead of years), cost $187,613, a cost only slightly less than a contemporary Ziegfeld production. The expense was clearly worthwhile, for the reception was ecstatic. Arthur Hornblow of *Theatre* exclaimed, "Such ravishingly beautiful tableaux, such gorgeous costumes, such a wealth of comedy and spectacular freshness, such a piling of Pelion on Ossa of everything that is decorative, dazzling, harmonious, intoxicatingly beautiful in the theatre—all that and more was handed out in a program that seemed to have no ending." In the *Times*, Alexander Woollcott waxed equally jubilant. He saw the producers of the "sumptuous bespangled revue" as "conjurors" who "pulled [out] all manner of gay tunes and brilliant trappings and funny clowns and nimble dancers." Later, becoming specific, he reported, "The new revue is ablaze with color—color wrought by Hassard Short into a kaleidoscope of chic and fantastic and bizarre designs with lovely curtains of black lace, with costumes of radiant pearls picked out against velvet blackness, with a hundred and one odd and conceitful costumes worked into gay designs."

The decision to place Short in charge was brave and perspicacious, for although he had never before staged a full-scale revue, his work on this series would quickly establish him as one of the most brilliant joiners of sketches, song, and spectacle. Actually, before he staged the first edition he had staged little indeed—only some mini-revues for vaudeville and three Broadway musicals. Short was born in England in 1877 and began his career as an actor in London. He came to America in 1901. Until 1919 he was awarded increasingly important supporting roles, including parts in such hits as *Peg o' My Heart* and *East Is West*. As notices for the first *Music Box Revue* suggested, early on he displayed his impeccable taste and gift for theatrical movement. However, he proceeded cautiously. Only several seasons later was his equally striking inventiveness to surface.

Of course, in the tradition of these annuals, gorgeous mannequins accentuated the scenic beauty. In the first edition, "The Legend of the Pearls," which Woollcott mentioned, was a high point, but in "Dining

Out" the models were dressed as the courses in a regal dinner, while in "Eight Notes" eight of the girls (including then unknown Miriam Hopkins) paraded as notes on a scale.

Two aging, admired comics, William Collier and Sam Bernard, provided much of the laughter, although they turned out to be merely a prelude to even greater clowns. Wilda Bennett (from the world of operetta), Paul Frawley, Joe Santley, and the Brox Sisters put over the songs.

And the songs were those Berlin had written for his own show. The hit of the first edition became the theme for the entire series and in a way it presaged the growing importance of the melodic side of these shows, for the song was "Say It with Music." Frawley and Miss Bennett introduced it. The lyric assured listeners that most girls preferred to be kissed to the strains of Chopin or Lizst, but it might just as well have added that most playgoers were coming to prefer revues that, besides making them laugh and pleasing their eyes, sent them out of the theatre humming. The two other best remembered songs from the first edition were tied in with dancing. "Everybody Step," sung in assertive, jazzy close harmony by the Brox Sisters, was an acknowledgment of the still flourishing "dancing craze" and an invitation to join in the often frenetic stepping. "They Call It Dancing" went a bit further, spoofing the lunatic marathon dances that had carried the craze to an absurd extreme.

The roster of players who appeared in the subsequent editions, players who according to critics were often at peak form, provides eloquent testimony to the excellences of the *Music Box Revues*. Rambunctious, leering Bobby Clark and his pudgy sidekick Paul McCullough, long-legged Charlotte Greenwood, sassy Phil Baker, nervous Frank Tinney, and the incomparable Fanny Brice led the comic section. Clark and McCullough's routines included one in which Clark agrees to wrestle with a bear, since he assumes the bear will really be McCullough in costume. Of course, the bear turns out to be the genuine article. Miss Brice presented another aspiring ballerina, another seductress, and a Yiddish immigrant who is even willing to launder Ku Klux Klan sheets if she can only remain in America. Clark and Miss Brice cavorted as a sex-hungry caveman Adam and a titillatingly coy

Eve. In the 1923–24 edition they were augmented by two of the funniest and most famous skits in the whole history of American musical revue. Robert Benchley appeared to deliver his lecture, "The Treasurer's Report," squirming through some embarrassing admissions of nitwit incompetence, while Santley, Baker and two other dapper, sophisticated males offered George S. Kaufman's picture of what would happen "If Men Played Cards as Women Do."

Singers included Grace LaRue, John Steel, Oscar Shaw, and Grace Moore. They helped popularize such Berlin standards as "Lady of the Evening" (for years supposedly Berlin's own favorite among his songs), "Pack Up Your Sins and Go to the Devil," and "Crinoline Days" (1922); "An Orange Grove in California" and "What'll I Do?" (1923); and "All Alone" (1924). Mountings of these numbers ranged from elaborate to surprisingly simple. As Steel and Miss Moore sauntered through a sunny California orange grove the grove suddenly melted away into a shower of orange lights and the audience was sprayed with orange perfume. For the "All Alone" number Shaw and Miss Moore, both dressed in white, sat beside white telephones on opposite sides of an otherwise darkened stage. In between these extremes was the background of moonlit rooftops against which Steel sang "Lady of the Evening."

Typical of the series' spectacles were the "Diamond Horseshoe" number in the 1922–23 edition and the "Maid of Mesh" scene in the 1923–24 edition. In the former the great heroines of opera paraded in costumes bespangled with diamonds (or reasonable facsimiles thereof). The train of Miss LaRue's Thais gown opened to carpet virtually the whole stage. The "Maid of Mesh" beauties promenaded in gowns of gold and silver mesh before a similar drop curtain. This scene alone was reputed to have cost $50,000.

For the last edition, John Murray Anderson was called in to replace Short. Short, ironically, was then hired to replace Anderson at the *Greenwich Village Follies.* (Anderson had been shouldered out of his own creation). For this final edition Anderson inexplicably resorted to one outmoded device by allowing Rip Van Winkle to come back to life to serve as compère and to have his tour of the modern world serve as a thread of plot.

Rising costs, which made retaining the elaborate show at so intimate a theatre as the Music Box untenable, coupled with Harris and Berlin's perception that the sun was setting on such annuals, brought the series to an end. Although some critics sensed a slight diminution of excellence in the last production, Baral was probably right when he observed that the series "opened on top—and shuttered on top."

The last of the major annuals was unquestionably the least. Artistically, Earl Carroll's *Vanities* opened at the bottom and remained there. The *Vanities* were, as Stanley Green has characterized them, a "blend of tastelessness, nudity, and overpowering spectacle." The man behind these "glorified burlesques" was born in Pittsburgh in 1893, came penniless to New York, where he took work at a music publisher and soon began writing some moderately successful songs for revues and musical comedies. The best known of his songs were probably "Isle D'Amour," which José Collins introduced in the *Ziegfeld Follies of 1913*, and the title song of Charlotte Greenwood's popular vehicle, *So Long Letty*. He next turned to producing non-musical plays, only a few of which triumphed over contemptuous dismissal by the critics. Tellingly, his most successful mounting of this sort was a sleazy tale of white slavery and degeneration, *White Cargo*. Throughout his producing career both he and his shows would be haled into court on morals and other charges, and he himself served a four-month prison sentence for perjury. The relative ease with which he mounted his productions and built his own palatial, art-deco theatre stemmed from his good fortune in coming upon and befriending William R. Edrington, a rich Texas oil man who shared his interests and general lack of taste and decorum.

From 1923 through 1932 every year except 1927 and 1929 saw a new *Vanities*, all but one of which ran at least six months. So whatever their artistic shortcomings, they clearly appealed to a sizable, if lowbrow audience. In 1929 and again in 1935, Carroll produced kindred revues which he called the *Earl Carroll Sketch Book*. He attempted with marked success to have the best of two worlds in 1933 when he combined a book show with a revue as *Murder at the Vanities*.

His spectacles were sometimes traditional, sometimes novel. One device featured in many of the editions was the "living curtain," in which largely undraped girls formed signficant parts of the drops. He was also fond of using see-through materials, including cellophane, to titillate playgoers. A brush with the law occurred when seemingly nude nymphs (actually dressed in flesh-colored tights) cavorted in an underwater scene.

A number of superior comics also romped through the *Vanities*. At one time or another Jimmy Savo, Jack Benny, Milton Berle, Ted Healy, and Helen Broderick lent their considerable talents, but the consensus was that the material was poor and the talents wasted. Only Joe Cook, who performed in three editions, and Patsy Kelly scored heavily. Sophie Tucker also appeared in one edition—and laid an egg.

Musically these revues were almost totally barren. Just two songs from them have lasted: "Good Night, Sweetheart" (1931) and Harold Arlen's early "I Gotta Right To Sing the Blues" (1932).

In 1940, a final edition, which was a three-week failure, nonetheless earned a special place in American theatrical annals, for it marked the first time on Broadway that performers used microphones and amplification. Contemporary critics, more conscientious than their later counterparts about maintaining high standards for truly and totally live theatre, lambasted Carroll for the innovation.

These, then, were the major rivals of Ziegfeld and his *Follies*. At heart, they were all "girlie shows," although they varied widely in approach, tone, and artistic merit. *The Passing Shows* and *The Music Box Revues* were basically Ziegfeldian in concept, although the latter series, performed in the tiny Music Box Theatre, and distinguished by Berlin's melodies and a pervasive sense of style and wit always outclassed the Shubert mountings. Aesthetically, the nadir was reached in the *Vanities*. However, their very lewdness suggested that they were possibly more attuned to the loosening moral climate of the 1920s than were the more traditional annuals. But it was the least girlie-oriented of the series, the *Scandals*, with their emphasis on jazz song and dance and their sometimes biting topical skits, which probably best exemplified the annual of the post World War I era and the hedonistic 1920s. Of course, other attempts were made to establish series. At least any number of revues, by including dates in their titles, suggested they hoped to return year after year. With very few exceptions they did not. The most interesting exception deserves some attention.

That exception was the *Blackbirds*, a revue series that featured all-black casts. To put it in proper perspective, we need to look briefly at some theatrical history. As mentioned earlier, *The Origin of the Cake Walk; or, Clorindy*, produced as an afterpiece on the Casino Roof in 1898, was the first show written by and cast with blacks to play before major white audiences. At the turn of the century several black musicals—again both written and performed by blacks—had short New York runs, mostly because of the comic art of Bert Williams and George Walker. What little vogue they enjoyed soon faded, and for many years black musicals disappeared from the scene. It took the sparks from *Shuffle Along*, a 1921 musical comedy, to rekindle the rage for black musicals. Next to *Shuffle Along* the most successful black musical comedy was *Runnin' Wild*, a 1923 hit that left behind the quintessential dance number of the era, "The Charleston." The earlier shows were all book musicals, but with the revival of interest in black musicals coinciding with the height of revue's popularity both black musical comedies and black revues were produced. In another change, some of the material provided for these shows, while black-inspired, was white-written. As a rule the black revues were somewhat less successful, although they proved invaluable training grounds for many black talents. Several of these revues were produced by Lew Leslie, a white vaudevillian and night-club manager, who moved to Broadway, where his career as a producer was devoted almost entirely to mounting black entertainments. In 1922 he had offered *The Plantation Revue* and in 1924, *Dixie to Broadway*. He first produced a *Blackbirds* in London in 1926. Two years later he brought *Blackbirds of 1928* to New York. It was a smash hit, its record of 518 performances making it the longest running black musical of the decade.

But *Blackbirds of 1928* was hardly all black. Its music was by Jimmy McHugh and its lyrics by Dorothy Fields, who also contributed sketches. Costumes were by Kiviette. Of course, the popular black orchestrator and composer Will Vodery helped orchestrate the score, and on stage some leading black talent was part of the totally black cast. Adelaide Hall and Bill "Bojangles" Robinson are the best remembered.

Settings were attractive but extremely simple, often little more than drapes and a far cry from the often staggering opulence of older revues. Comedy was routine and so stereotypical that the show's black comedians were required to don the expected blackface to put across the humor. What really made the show was its superb dancing and its knockout score, which the performers offered with a zest that was perceived throughout the era as uniquely characteristic of black entertainments. "I Can't Give You Anything But Love" was the biggest hit of the evening, although "Diga Diga Do" and "Doin' the New Low Down" were also show stoppers. To the extent that music was a salient feature of the revue, *Blackbirds of 1928* was another of the handful of 1920s' revues that pointed assuredly toward the future.

Subsequent American editions of the revue—in 1930, 1933, and 1939—all failed, though the 1930 version left behind Eubie Blake's "Memories of You." Parenthetically, the series was a rarity in that it was transatlantic, and, while no edition approached the popularity of the 1928 mounting, London editions in 1934 and 1936 enjoyed modest successes.

However, by the 1930s annuals were patently obsolescent if not yet totally obsolete. The best theatrical craftsmen had studied the lessons taught by the more avant-garde revues of the 1920s and had consolidated their art to such a degree that the new decade would soon come to be looked on as a halcyon time for the more thoughtful, melodic revue.

6

On the Band Wagon

On the last day of April 1929—just six months before Wall Street collapsed, taking with it an era and much of that era's theatre—a revue opened at the Music Box Theatre. The show was not another *Music Box Revue*. That wonderful series had been consigned to the shelf four years earlier. Instead the revue had a rather unusual title for Broadway. Shunning ballyhoo and grandiloquence, it was called, simply and refreshingly, *The Little Show*. It was anything but little in merit and importance, for it really began the long line of smart, superior connoisseur revues that were among the great delights of Broadway in the troubled thirties. Brooks Atkinson grasped something of its significance when he opened his notice, "Most of the wit, humor and intelligence that somehow escape the musical stage has settled down pleasantly into 'The Little Show,' which rambled along in conversational tones at the Music Box last evening. It is unfailingly diverting."

There was no denying the show's "wit, humor and intelligence." Even today its most famous sketch reads hilariously. But then it was the work of a master, George S. Kaufman. "The Still Alarm" was a delicious send-up of that sense of order and decorum which lent a special polish to the period's glittering façades. Set in a burning hotel it described the impeccable coolness and the studious good manners of two well-bred businessmen and two firemen who come to rescue them. One of the firemen is a frustrated violinist who carries his violin with him wherever he goes, and the sketch ends with a sedate, smoky, impromptu concert. The businessmen were played by Clifton Webb and Romney Brent; one of the firemen was Fred Allen. Until this show Webb had been a sauve song and dance man, often featured but never starred, while Allen was a rising vaudeville comic, who also had never seen his name above the title.

The show's music was equally good, although this seems not to have been apparent at the time. In another connection, Alan Jay Lerner has said that a musical's book makes a show a success, but its music decides whether the show will endure. Of course, given the topical or ephemeral nature of so many revue skits, the same cannot hold true entirely for revues. Yet in the case of *The Little Show*, with the possibly noteworthy exception of "The Still Alarm," it is the revue's best songs which have endured and helped keep its reputation alive. First-nighters roundly applauded at least two songs, "Can't We Be Friends?," written by Kay Swift and her banker husband James Warburg, who published under the name Paul James, and "Moanin' Low," which lyricist Howard Dietz wrote with composer Ralph Rainger, and which gave Webb and Libby Holman, the revue's third star, a real show-stopper. With time, however, another song from the evening has come to the forefront, Dietz and Arthur Schwartz's "I Guess I'll Have To Change My Plan." All the songs have a certain introverted quality as opposed to the more brash, gusty, or pontifical songs so dear to the huge annuals. This, along with their often more extended melodic lines and burnished harmonies, reflected newer approaches to popular song and hinted at the crooning style just beginning to come into vogue.

Whether or not the producers of *The Little Show* had originally envisaged a new series is moot, but the success of the revue certainly planted the idea in their heads. Unfortunately, *The Second Little Show* and *The Third Little Show*, mounted in the two following years, were not up to the mark, although the 1931 show had Beatrice Lillie and Ernest Truex as stars and offered such songs as "When Yuba Plays the Rhumba on the Tuba," "There Are Fairies at the Bottom of My Garden," and Noel Coward's "Mad Dogs and Englishmen."

Schwartz and Dietz contributed most of the score to the second edition. Nothing they created for the show proved popular, but at the same time they contributed songs for another revue, much on the order of *The Little Show*, which scored a huge success and helped propel them into the front ranks of revue songwriters.

Dietz was born in New York in 1896 and had a remarkably varied career. For over thirty years he was director of publicity for MGM Pictures, where he was credited with having devised the famous lion trademark and its slogan. Jerome Kern first brought him to Broadway to be the lyricist for a failed 1924 musical, *Dear Sir*. In 1927 he contributed lyrics to the revue *Merry-Go-Round*. Schwartz was born in Brooklyn in 1900. He had been trained as a lawyer, but, although he later helped ASCAP in legal capacities, soon realized he preferred composing. *The Little Show* was his first score. By late 1930, when Dietz and he turned to the new revue, he had six Broadway and London shows to his credit.

That revue came about in no small measure because when the producers of *The Little Show* cast the second edition they foolishly elected to jettison their stars. Max Gordon, a vaudeville booker then just embarking on a career as a Broadway producer, quickly signed them up, at the same time enlisting Hassard Short to stage the work. Although he called the revue *Three's a Crowd*, his trio of stars were delightful company and with Short's stylish assistance turned the entertainment into an evening crowded only with pleasure. The iconoclastic opening set the tone for the evening's excellent comedy. Instead of a brassy, high-kicking song and dance the curtain rose to reveal a bedroom and the action suggested the beginning of a naughty French farce. But just as the husband was about to discover his wife's lover under a bed stagehands whisked away the bed, and Fred Allen appeared to assure audiences this would not be a night of bawdy escapades. Only then did the chorus jump out to ask, "What will we do for blackouts?" Yet however witty and visually appealing the revue was, its excellences were again capped by a superb score. Miss Holman had three applause-getters to sing, "Yaller" (by Richard Myers and Charles Schwab), "Body and Soul" (by Johnny Green, Frank Eyton, Edward Heyman, and Robert Sour), and Schwartz and Dietz's "Something To Remember You By." The dance that followed her singing of "Body and Soul" was one of the evening's most unforgettable moments. She had sung the number close to the footlights, which went dark on her exit. The curtains then opened on a totally unlit, black-draped stage. Two eerie green lights came up slowly to reveal the silhouettes of Webb and Tamara Geva, who began a sinuous, sensuous routine. All during the dance small spotlights focused at times on their hands, at times on their feet, at times on their torsos with dramatic suggestiveness. More than one critic felt the lighting was at least as imaginative as the dance.

Three's a Crowd opened in October 1930 and might have been the season's best revue had not another entry appeared just as the season was closing. Like the first *Little Show* and *Three's a Crowd*, its songwriters were Schwartz and Dietz, who this time wrote all the songs. They were at peak form, as was everyone else connected with the show, so *The Band Wagon* is now recalled as one of, arguably the very greatest of American revues. The songwriters were reunited for this effort with producer Max Gordon and director Hassard Short, as well as *Three's a Crowd*'s set designer and costume designer, Albert Johnson and Kiviette. A five-star cast was headed by Fred and Adele Astaire (her Broadway farewell), Helen Broderick, Frank Morgan, and Tilly Losch. Moreover, to give the show a certain consistency of style and tone, not only were no interpolated songs allowed but all the sketches were by George S. Kaufman or Dietz.

Robert Garland of the *World-Telegram* judged the results "pretty nearly perfect," adding, "It has humor and restraint, beauty and sophistication, taste and timeliness."

Visually the show was a knockout. The settings' beauties were enhanced by a major change in lighting practices, for footlights were eliminated and much of the principal illumination came from lamps hung in front of the balcony. Standard practice now, it was then a novelty. Moreover, Johnson's double revolving stage allowed not merely for swift scene changes but sometimes became a partner in the action. Most famous of all was the ornate old-world merry-go-round which spun the cast as it sang "I Love Louisa." But the turning stage was used to equal effect in the ballet "The Beggar Waltz," in which Astaire, as a beggar who haunts the stage door of the Vienna Opera House, falls asleep and dreams he dances with the ravishing prima ballerina (Miss Losch) for one gala evening, only to wake from his dream just as she leaves the theatre. Similarly, the Astaires, as two Parisian brats, set the French capital spinning with their mischievous antics in "Hoops." Their "Hoops" exit was their famous "runaround" in which they scurried in ever larger arcs until they disappeared into the wings. In "White Heat" both were dressed in top hats, white ties, and tails and danced together before a modernistic black-and-silver setting resembling a huge, wide smoke stack, all the while a similarly top-hatted, be-tailed chorus stepped in tricky counterpoint.

Novelty was underscored from the very first curtain, which was no curtain at all, since arriving playgoers saw on stage a seeming mirror image of the very auditorium they were filling. The company, all dolled up like traditional first-nighters of the period, took seats on stage, browsed through programs, and insisted that what followed had "better be good." Later, raked, mirrored floors, reflecting ever-changing lighting patterns, were the platform on which Tilly Losch interpreted "Dancing in the Dark."

While none of Kaufman's or Dietz's sketches proved as enduring as some of Kaufman's earlier skits, such as "If Men Played Cards As Women Do" or "The Still Alarm," the best were of exceptionally high caliber. In "For Good Old Nectar" collegiate cheerleaders jumped and shouted not for some sports hero but for the winner of a history prize. As a fashionable shopper in "Pour le Bain," Miss Broderick was confronted by a salesman determined to show every plumbing fixture was a veritable work of modern art. When she insisted on being given a demonstration of one, the salesman's cavalier reply was "Heard melodies are sweet, but those unheard are sweeter." Topping the fun was "The Pride of the Claghornes." Colonel and Mrs. Claghorne are prepared to toast the engagement of their daughter, Breeze, to Carter Simpson, when the Simpsons announce they will not permit the wedding to take place. Their reasoning is irrefutable—Breeze is rumored to be a virgin. The Colonel, aghast at Breeze's disgraceful, un-Southern behavior, orders his daughter from his house and the bereaved parents are left to bemoan, "I just can't understand this modern generation." Morgan and Miss Broderick portrayed the Claghornes, the Astaires the ill-starred young couple.

Once again, however, the passage of time has suggested that the music was the crowning jewel of the evening. Schwartz created one of the greatest of all revue scores. The standout was, of course, "Dancing in the Dark," followed closely by "High and Low," "New Sun in the Sky," and the witty "Confession," as well as other songs already mentioned.

Although *The Band Wagon* was a far cry from the heavily ornate, more leisurely paced extravaganzas of Ziegfeld's day, it played, not inappropriately, at the very New Amsterdam Theatre where the *Ziegfeld Follies* had flourished in their heyday. Ironically, a month after the show opened Ziegfeld brought forth the last edition of the *Follies* which he was to supervise personally. With the New Amsterdam booked, he offered it at his own Ziegfeld Theatre, the only edition to play there.

A year later many of the same figures who had put together *Three's a Crowd* and *The Band Wagon* tried again with *Flying Colors*. Gordon was the producer, Dietz wrote most of the sketches, with assists from Kaufman and others, and Schwartz and Dietz created the songs. Another fine cast was headed this time by Clifton Webb, Charles Butterworth, Tamara Geva, and Patsy Kelly, with Vilma and Buddy Ebsen, Larry Adler, and Imogene Coca among the supporting players. The revue was a success and not without merit, but it had a certain less than fresh quality to it. Critics felt that many of the numbers were consciously imitative of the hits from earlier revues. For example, "Meine Kleine Akrobat" echoed the oompah beat of "I Love Louisa," while "Alone Together" seemed an attempt to recapture the sultry ardor of "Body and Soul." The show's best numbers were its liveliest, "A Shine on Your Shoes" and "Louisiana Hayride."

So it remained for Irving Berlin to spearhead the next great revue, one which ranks close to *The Band Wagon* as a masterpiece of the 1930s. In one way *As Thousands Cheer* might be seen as a small throwback to the days when revues had plots or at least themes, for the entire show purported to be a living newspaper (a phrase Depression dramatists were to grab hold of), with its headlines coming alive in songs and sketches. The sketches were by Moss Hart. His comic slices of life and Berlin's songs were performed by a superb company headed by Marilyn Miller (ending her career, as she began it, in a revue), Clifton Webb, Ethel Waters, and Helen Broderick.

The show opened with a brief skit in which a Park Avenue husband is bitten by his wife's Pekingese and bites it back. The "Man Bites Dog" headline set the presses and the show rolling. For the remaining skits Hart had recourse to famous names of the day, beginning with a retiring President Hoover, who is persuaded by his wife to tell the members of his outgoing cabinet what he really thinks of them. He does, first offering Secretary of State Stimson a Bronx cheer. The Joan Crawford-Douglas Fairbanks, Jr., divorce (with Miss Miller and Webb as proxies) degenerates into a squabble over publicity rights to the divorce. Matters become moot when Fairbanks Sr.'s divorce from Mary Pickford usurps the headlines. Webb was next forced to age rapidly to impersonate a 94-year-old John D. Rockefeller refusing a gift of Rockefeller Center. Less successful was Miss Waters's comic wife of an actor whose single line in *The Green Pastures* has inflated his ego. Metropolitan Opera broadcasts were mocked with a *Rigoletto* regularly interrupted for commercials. A contest in one-upmanship between Mahatma Gandhi and Aimee Semple McPherson (read Webb and Miss Broderick) ends with their forming a dance team to promote the sale of religion. Miss Miller, Miss Waters, and Webb demonstrated Noel Coward's uplifting influence on the behavior of hotel staffs, while a final skit touched on rumors that the Prince of Wales might marry.

Among the notable musical numbers were two performed by Miss Waters, the lively "Heat Wave" and the poignant tale of a black woman whose husband has been lynched, "Supper Time." The presentations were a study in contrasts. In the first the gaiety imbued everything, even

Miss Waters's sizzlingly colored full-length, full-sleeved gown with a matching hat that looked like a warped dunce cap. Punctuating the costume were her huge earrings. She belted out the song surrounded by a chorus in equally gaudy get-ups, then moved aside to let José Limon and other dancers have their turn at the song. Her costume for "Supper Time" was simple and drab, with a mournful black bandana on her head. The scene was set in a shabby room, where she prepared to set the table for herself and her children. She also saluted Josephine Baker in "Harlem on My Mind." The first-act finale began with a tableau done entirely in the sepia tones of the period's rotogravure sections. The scene harked back fifty years to depict Fifth Avenue during an 1883 "Easter Parade," and as movement suddenly animated the picture the cast sang what became the hit of the show. The second act's finale was a little novel, beginning with the Supreme Court handing down a decision that musicals could not end with reprises. So instead another superior Berlin song, "Not for All the Rice in China," closed the entertainment.

The show was designed by Albert Johnson and staged by Hassard Short, who had worked so skillfully on *The Band Wagon*. Short, of course, had also staged many of the *Music Box Revues*, and since the revue was produced by Sam Harris at the Music Box, the show was an incomparable amalgam of echoes of a not-so-distant past with the best in contemporary revue. It ran nearly a year, a long run at the height of the Depression.

None of the four superior revues to premiere in 1934 ran nearly as long, probably because none had the consistency of style, tone, and wit, nor the overall excellence of *As Thousands Cheer*. Two of the shows appeared during the 1933–34 season, as had the Berlin-Hart entertainment; the other two opened early in the 1934–35 season. First to arrive was the *Ziegfeld Follies of 1934*. A claim could be made that this was simply the latest in that beloved old series. Indeed, playgoers who believed everything they read might have been lead into undue expectations by the announcement that the new edition had been produced by Mrs. Florenz Ziegfeld (better known as Billie Burke). Certainly, they would have reasoned, she could be expected to maintain her husband's lofty traditions. What they may not have known is that Mrs. Ziegfeld was desperately trying to pay off the enormous debts the late producer had left behind and so had entrusted the production to the Shuberts. But the only illustrious names the Shuberts recalled from the glamorous heyday of the *Follies* were Fanny Brice and costume designer Charles LeMaire. Much of Miss Brice's comedy harked back to the types and styles she satirized in bygone years. As "Soul-Saving Sadie" (from Avenue A) she ridiculed the Aimee Semple McPherson variety of commercialized religion; she took off nudists who take off all their clothes in "Sunshine Sarah"; and lamented the plight of the impoverished Countess Dubinsky ("now she strips for Minsky"), presenting a riotously bumpy bump and grind strip tease in the process. But she also introduced the character which would later consolidate her fame on radio, Baby Snooks. Dressed in a short, heavily starched smock, she first presented her precocious, prevaricating brat in a skit in which her exasperated parents attempt to put an end to her constant lying by telling her the story of George Washington and the cherry tree. Snooks listens with a smile of cynical innocence, then goes right on lying. Some playgoers saw the character as a variation of the rambunctious little devil that Ray Dooley had brought to life so hilariously in the teens and the twenties, and they were right. But Miss Dooley had depended heavily on wildly physical fun (for example, scampering across seats and passengers in a railroad car), while Miss Brice's monster was more verbal. Willie and Eugene Howard, two stalwarts from the Shuberts' defunct *Passing Shows* and later from *George White's Scandals*, were also signed on. The rest of the performers, writers, and designers were generally from a newer order. Singers Jane Froman and Everett Marshall and the song and dance team of Vilma and Buddy Ebsen were allotted important chores. Lyricists included E. Y. Harburg, Edward Heyman, Ballard MacDonald, and Billy Rose. Among the composers were Vernon Duke, Peter DeRose, and James F. Hanley. MacDonald and Hanley were represented by their 1919 hit "Rose of Washington Square," which Miss Brice revived for the occasion. However, the hits of the show were two Western-style numbers, Billy Hill's "The Last Roundup" and Hill and De Rose's "Wagon Wheels." Settings were by Watson

Barratt, a Shubert workhorse who had created many of the sets for *The Passing Shows*, and by the designer of *The Band Wagon*, Albert Johnson. Costumes were by Kiviette. Their designs were apparently excellent, although reading between the lines of critical praise one senses a loss at the omission of Joseph Urban from the roster. While not the original director, it was John Murray Anderson who whipped the final version into shape. Brooks Atkinson slyly balanced merits and demerits by reporting the show "the best edition of the 'Ziegfeld Follies' the Shuberts ever put on stage." The show played the Shuberts' Winter Garden, where the *Passing Shows* had once reigned and where all subsequent *Follies* would appear.

If the *Follies* essentially was a longing look backward, *New Faces* attempted its own glimpse into the future by emphasizing the fresh talents striving for a place in the theatrical spotlight. The conception was not entirely original. As early as 1923 a failed revue called *The Newcomers* had employed the same approach. Indeed, in another very small way, *New Faces* looked backward, for, nominally at least, it was produced by Ziegfeld's greatest rival, Charles Dillingham, himself now bankrupt and dying. Another oldtimer, Elsie Janis, worked behind the scenes. However, the real moving force behind the revue was Leonard Sillman, who had first mounted the work as *Low and Behold* in Pasadena. The evening was filled with pleasant if unexceptional sketches and equally pleasant if unexceptional songs. The show's claims to fame come from the fact that it inaugurated an intermittent but often successful series of a basically new type—with its emphasis on unknowns—and that from this edition came Imogene Coca (who was hardly making her debut, having been around for nearly a decade), Henry Fonda, Sillman himself, and Nancy Hamilton. Miss Hamilton wrote many of the sketches and lyrics as well as performing in the musical. Later she would produce some highly successful revues on her own, and John Murray Anderson would call her "the wittiest and ablest revue writer in America."

Despite shortcomings, the most successful of the 1934 revues was *Life Begins at 8:40*. Its own life began when it was projected as another edition of the *Follies*, with John Murray Anderson contemplating a production done almost entirely in white. The novel idea was intriguing but fundamentally unworkable and was soon dropped. So was the idea of another *Follies* when some legal problems emerged. Since Anderson was in on this show from the start he was given a freer hand and, apparently, a somewhat larger budget to work with. He enlisted Albert Johnson for the settings and a long line of costume designers, including Kiviette, James Reynolds and Raoul Pène duBois. Johnson devised an interesting variation on the revolving stages with which he was becoming identified. For *Life Begins at 8:40* he created two concentric platforms, which turned in opposite directions. The musical opened with the inner stage supporting a huge clock while masked performers on the outer stage represented the stereotypical revue types—the old-fashioned clown, the more sophisticated comedian, the handsome tenor, the lithe dancer. As they revolved the chorus sang, "At exactly eighty-forty or thereabout, the little play world . . . comes to life." Among the other settings and costumes singled out were those for "Spring Fever," with its golden hues, and the charming period picture, not unlike that used in *As Thousands Cheer*'s "Easter Parade" number, for "What Can You Say in a Love Song?"

The cast was first-rate, headed by Ray Bolger, Bert Lahr, Luella Gear, and Frances Williams. Since some critics suggested their material wasn't as good as the settings and costumes, Bolger came off best. After all, he depended less on melodies and words than he did on his two nimble feet. With Dixie Dunbar he put across the evening's most popular song, "You're a Builder-Upper," but he also had fun teasing an orchestra that couldn't keep time with his eccentric rhythms and in a dumb-show version of a prizefight. The caterwauling Lahr made much of little when he impersonated a pompous tea-concert singer gushing at the "utter, utter, utter loveliness of things" (it earned him a pie in his face), and portraying his celebrated stage Englishman, a suicidal Frenchman, and a gullible Wall Street client. The sardonic Miss Gear delighted with her saga of a forlorn spinster, "I Couldn't Hold My Man." Although Harold Arlen wrote the score to lyrics by Ira Gershwin and E. Y. Harburg, they were none of them quite at top form. But the excellence of the production and the stars' diverse talents saw to it that their second best was good enough to keep the show on the boards for seven months.

Two days after Christmas Eddie Dowling presented *Thumbs Up*, a potpourri that was the work of no fewer than fifteen writers and featured a huge cast of favorites, which included his wife, Ray Dooley, as well as Bobby Clark and Paul McCullough, Hal LeRoy, Paul Draper, and Jack Cole. Dowling turned to the seemingly ubiquitous John Murray Anderson to stage the entertainment. Anderson in turn selected a relative unknown, Ted Weidhass, for settings and such old dependables as James Reynolds and Raoul Pène duBois for the clothes. Typical of their work was the opening number, "Skating in Central Park," which appealed to the perennial craving for nostalgia with its Currier and Ives-like look at a bygone New York.

Burns Mantle, one of the better critics who was captivated by the show, was especially happy that the comedy was "cleaner" than that in many other revues. It remained a toss-up whether Bobby Clark or Miss Dooley came away with top honors. Clark's best moment was as a microphone-hogging judge in a broadcast trial, while the irrepressible comedienne resorted to some of her acrobatic antics to become the apex of a human pyramid of Arabs and to scamper over the backs of her entourage as the prima donna in a spoof of *The Merry Widow*.

The two songs from the show that were soon hummed far and wide were James Hanley's "Zing! Went the Strings of My Heart" and Vernon Duke's "Autumn in New York."

Given the many delighted notices it received, the popularity of its performers and the great success of two of its songs, its twenty-week run was a distinct disappointment. Quite possibly word of mouth supported those dissenting critics—such as Atkinson of the influential *Times*—who felt it pleased the eye more than it did the soul.

It might be argued that *Thumbs Up* would have enjoyed a longer run had it opened earlier in the season, since, with no air-conditioning to comfort playgoers, it closed with the coming of warm weather. But apparently, for all their excellences, a certain sameness was creeping into revues. Moreover, the 1934 crop introduced relatively little in the way of memorable music compared with scores earlier in the decade.

But 1935 was no better. Indeed, though six of the ten musicals to debut in that year were revues, only two or three could be considered successes and all were outclassed by the best book shows—*Porgy and Bess*, *Jubilee*, and *Jumbo*. Somewhat perversely, one of the failed revues, *Provincetown Follies*, left behind the enduring "Red Sails in the Sunset," while one of the comparative successes, the 1936 edition of *George White's Scandals* (it opened Christmas night, 1935), offered nothing of distinction. The Theatre Guild, which had presented playgoers with the beguiling *Garrick Gaieties*, came a cropper when it brought out *Parade*, a revue dismissed angrily by some critics as too stridently left-wing to be real fun.

The longest running of 1935's revues was the *Earl Carroll Sketch Book*, another of that producer's low-brow hodge-podges which found enough ticket-buyers to play just over six months. By far the best revue of the year, however, ran only a week less, suggesting the philistines did not greatly outnumber Broadway's more discriminating playgoers. *At Home Abroad* was a Shubert offering, designed to play the huge Winter Garden. It had songs by Schwartz and Dietz and sketches by Dietz and Marc Connelly, among others. Its settings and costumes were by its brilliant young co-director, Vincente Minnelli. A superb cast was headed by two great ladies of the American musical theatre, Beatrice Lillie and Ethel Waters, who were supported by a glittering list of associates including Vera Ellen, Eddie Foy, Jr., Reginald Gardiner, Paul Haakon, Eleanor Powell, and Herb Williams.

Quite possibly because the often tradition-bound Shuberts were bankrolling the show it took a marked leap backwards by returning to the idea that a revue should have a plot. But that plot—a couple's tour of the world—was so slim it never got in the way of the fun, leading John Mason Brown to call it "as pleasant and profitable a world cruise as any stay-at-home could invest in."

The cruise was filled with visual delights. Minnelli's palette was rich in light, bright colors, many of them pastels. They had an exhilarating freshness to them. But if his colors had a flowing logic, theatrical exigencies saw to it that Minnelli's tourists jumped all over the map in a way no real tourist could have in a pre-jet era (and indeed the tourists were forgotten by the end of the last act). For example, between watching Miss Lillie try to purchase two dozen double damask dinner napkins at a London department store (a skit originally done by Cicely Courtneidge in the 1928 London revue, *Clowns in Clover*) and watching her step from a gigantic travel poster to sing of "Paree" ("kees zee Bois—oooh, kees Montparnasse!"), they were whisked to an Africa where Ethel Waters, dressed in thick gold bands and a blue, star-spangled gown, ruled as a snazzy "Hottentot Potentate." In another bit of far-flung exotica she introduced "The Steamboat Whistle" while a chorus hidden behind black rubber Jamaican masks pranced around her. Miss Waters, too, was transported to Paris, where, bedecked in gold lamé, she sulked in her posh suite while wailing a torchy lament, "Thief in the Night." Other highlights were Miss Lillie's instructing playgoers to "Get Yourself a Geisha" (insisting "It's better with your shoes off"), Reginald Gardiner's hilarious monologue in which wallpaper and trains become almost human, and Miss Powell's scintillating tap dancing, including the "That's Not Cricket" number in which she and the chorus stepped gaily, all the while dressed in Etonian high hats, short jackets with huge Buster Brown collars, and striped pants.

One skit from the show, a skit which has not entered the canon of revue classics, but which was made side-splitting at the time by Miss Lillie's antics, was "The Audience Waits." The comedienne was seen as a great Russian ballerina who is refusing to perform until her lover returns to her. While her audience waits for her and she waits for her lover, she reminisces about her early years—her tribulations in a largely impoverished czarist land ("I could not face the muzhik"), her constant trekking, trekking, now at last ended since "you can't teach an old dog new treks." When her manager urgently asks, "You won't dance?," her reply is "Don't ask me." Her lover finally arrives, so she rushes on stage, blissfully unaware this gives her man an opportunity to make a play for her understudy. Even when some of the material in the sketch was less than top drawer, Miss Lillie dipped into her seemingly inexhaustible bag of tricks for the gesture, the glance, or the intonation that made it uproarious. She could assume a pose with all the haughty grace of a Pavlova, then scratch her behind to shatter the illusion. If playgoers laughed loudly at one of the puns she would turn and glower at them in such pretended outrage that they only laughed some more. On the line "Don't ask me" she injected just enough melody to remind listeners the line was stolen from a then popular Kern-Hammerstein-Fields song. Her singular juxtaposition of vulgarity and absurdity on the one hand and lordliness on the other was the crux of her unique genius. Not for nothing did she call her autobiography *Every Other Inch a Lady.*

Apart from the comic numbers, no enduring classic emerged from the Schwartz-Dietz collaboration, although "Farewell, My Lovely," "Got a Bran' New Suit," and "Love Is a Dancing Thing" could not be readily dismissed.

The Shuberts, Minnelli, and Miss Lillie were to be reunited just over a year later for the most successful of 1936's revues, *The Show Is On,* but before that reached the Winter Garden's stage on Christmas night two other noteworthy revues had preceded it.

The first of these was the 1936 edition of the *Ziegfeld Follies.* Once again the Shuberts were the real producers, although as in 1934 they gave Mrs. Florenz Ziegfeld public credit. And once again the Shuberts assembled an impressive array of talent, including Vernon Duke and Ira Gershwin for the songs, John Murray Anderson for the staging, Robert Alton and George Balanchine for the dances, and Vincente Minnelli for the sets and costumes. David Freedman, who had written the original "Baby Snooks" skit, wrote virtually all the dialogue. Bob Hope, Gertrude Niesen, Harriet Hoctor, Eve Arden, and Judy Canova were among the capable players performing in support of the stars, Fanny Brice and, after a long sojourn in Europe, Josephine Baker.

Miss Baker was the only major disappointment in an evening most critics felt surpassed the 1934 Shubert–Billie Burke edition. For many, top honors went to Minnelli, with Atkinson noting, "Although he is lavish enough to satisfy any producer's thirst for opulence, his taste is unerring and the 'Follies' that comes off his drawing-board is a civilized institution." At one point he dressed the girls in cellophane, a trick Earl Carroll had used much earlier but without Minnelli's impeccable taste. Harking back still further, he created for "Island in the West Indies" another of the explosions of lush tropical colorings that had been a standby since the very earliest *Follies.*

There was also little question that Miss Brice walked away with performing honors. She spoofed British accents and mannerisms in "Fancy Fancy," kidded her own singing of "My Man" by leaning against a lamp post to deliver "He Hasn't a Thing Except Me" (she soon hadn't even the lamp post, which quickly moved off to the wings), and with cross-eyed intensity preached "Rewolt! Rewolt!" Few playgoers who laughed at her "Baby Snooks Goes Hollywood" could foresee that she herself was about to join the trek westward and that this would be her last Broadway appearance.

Hope and Miss Arden sang the revue's best song, "I Can't Get Started."

The show was so dependent on Miss Brice that when she took ill in the spring it was forced to close. When she recovered the revue reopened in the fall with Bobby Clark, Jane Pickens, and Gypsy Rose Lee as major additions to the cast.

Although New Faces of 1936 ran nearly half a year its major attractions were not its newcomers—even if Van Johnson went on to Hollywood stardom—but rather Imogene Coca, who was held over from the original edition, and the Duncan Sisters, who had been theatrical favorites for two decades. Like most of the series this edition was often witty and chic, and like most of the series it left nothing of enduring merit behind.

By the time The Show Is On sent first-nighters scurrying back to the Winter Garden, many a playgoer must have come to perceive the theatre as the home of the best revues of the period, which it often had been. Indeed, for a while it was to revues what earlier the New Amsterdam had been. The Show Is On would bring the best of that tradition to an end, even if several later revues would enjoy longer runs at the house than any of the more stylish potpourris of the 1930s.

Once more the Shuberts, with their traditionalist instincts, returned to the old gimmick of a theme—this time show business around the world. And once more the Shuberts signed on a marvelous selection of Broadway's finest talents, with David Freedman and Moss Hart creating the sketches, Dietz, Lorenz Hart, E. Y. Harburg, and Ira Gershwin among the lyricists, and Schwartz, Hoagy Carmichael, Vernon Duke, Richard Rodgers, Harold Arlen and George Gershwin writing the melodies. Bert Lahr joined Miss Lillie to add their inimitable humor to the shenanigans. And what shenanigans they were! With a new monicker, Ronald Traylor, and a widow's peak down to his eyebrows, Lahr was transformed into a popular matinee idol sent to lure away a Baltimore divorcée from the king who would give up his throne for her. He spoofed modern swing singers, squeaking eagerly, snapping his fingers, and offering his own scat of "Winny, winny, winny, winny, woo-hoo" (not to mention "gnong-gnong"). With mock solemnity and gusto he caterwauled (more "gnong-gnong") his way through "Song of the Woodman," a lumberjack proudly cataloguing the final products of his labors ("Seats all shapes and classes / For little lads and little lasses"). Miss Lillie, using the name Gogo Benuti and bedeviled by a large corsage of orchids, also took a turn at twitting rhythm singers. In a send-up of Josephine Baker and her often wispy ways, she found hilarious subterfuges for sneaking peeks when she was supposed to be asleep. Parodying generations of treacly moon songs, she swung out over the audience while seated on a crescent moon, threw garters at the men and cried, "I ain't had no lovin' since January, February— Gawd knows when!" In the guise of a great actress who is told her next play is "about a man and woman," she dismisses it out of hand for "too much plot." With both Leslie Howard and John Gielgud offering their Hamlets in nearby theatres, Miss Lillie portrayed a pesky playgoer arriving late and making troublesome comments at the Gielgud version (Gielgud was impersonated by Reginald Gardiner.) When the unnerved Gielgud-Gardiner offers to buy her a ticket to Howard's interpretation, Miss Lillie revealed Howard had bought her the ticket for Gielgud. (Gardiner had his best solo moment mimicking a Stokowski-like prima donna conductor.) The stars combined to devastate *Uncle Tom's Cabin*, with Lahr as Tom and Miss Lillie as Little Eva, and to recall bump and grind burlesque with Lahr as a red-nosed buffoon and Miss Lillie as the leading stripper (given the possibilities in this number it is amazing how many critics passed over it).

Perhaps more surprising, critics who praised Minnelli nonetheless gave his designs and direction little real attention. They might call it "a luminous work of art" with "a procession of soft and winning splendours," but they were niggardly in providing details. To an extent, the same thing had happened to Joseph Urban. Such consistently outstand-ing artistry again came to be taken for granted. Perhaps, too, there was a growing feeling that however admirable such tasteful spectacle was, it no longer represented an essential feature. For though the critics also knew they could take for granted the comic gifts of the stars, they showered them with praise and description.

The revue's best songs included the Gershwins' salute to the waltz, "By Strauss," and a charming if atypical Carmichael tune, "Little Old Lady."

More than one critic proclaimed the revue the best that had ever played the Winter Garden. So in its way the show was a glorious swan song for an era and a particular type of revue—a revue that combined something of Ziegfeldian glamour with the wit, melody, and pacing of later innovators.

In the new year which followed the Shuberts' beguiling Christmas gift, the theatrical road reached a turning. Revues were never to be quite the same again.

7

Whatzapoppin

In his engaging study of 1930s' musicals, *Ring Bells! Sing Songs!*, theatrical historian Stanley Green has written of 1937, "More sharply than did any other year, it pitted the old versus the new." This applied to musicals in general as well as to some aspects of the non-musical theatre, but it most certainly applied to revues in a peculiar and even alarming way.

Although some critics insisted that Ed Wynn's inability to develop a character and hew to a story line turned *Hooray for What!* into another one of his zany hodgepodges, it still professed to be a book musical. The lone major musical arrival of 1937 unquestionably to follow traditional revue form was an almost sui generis breakaway show. *Pins and Needles* opened in a theatre that had long since left the theatrical mainstream. Its cast was made up of performers who were not only unknown to playgoers but who were not even professional actors. Nor were the writers, with one exception, well known. And its producer was a name not heretofore seen in mastheads. For *Pins and Needles* began life as a showcase for a union, its talented members and its political outlook. The union was the I.L.G.W.U., the International Ladies' Garment Workers Union, operating as the Labor Stage.

The show had its genesis several years earlier when songwriter Harold Rome created topical songs for entertainments at a Jewish summer resort. These songs came to the attention of a man who was in charge of theatrical activities for the union. At first union members balked at the idea of mounting a revue, insisting they preferred more serious works, but they were eventually won over. Because the cast was recruited from the ranks of cutters, weavers, and others who normally worked forty hours a week, rehearsals had to spread out over far more than the customary four or five weeks. Meeting about three times a week, they took over a year and a half to whip the show into shape.

Since most of the cast had to work Monday through Friday and since no one apparently realized the success the show would enjoy, the first performances in June 1936 were slated only for Friday and Saturday evenings. Performances were given in a small studio above the tiny auditorium on 39th Street called the Labor Stage. The building served as an "Arts Center" for the I.L.G.W.U., but it had seen better days. Just over twenty years earlier it had been known as the Princess Theatre and had been home to the intimate musical comedies with which P. G. Wodehouse, Guy Bolton, and Jerome Kern had helped transform the American lyric theatre—the Princess Theatre shows such as *Very Good Eddie*; *Oh, Boy!*; and *Oh, Lady! Lady!!*. In the 1920s the theatre had also housed a number of interesting dramas.

At first no advertisements were placed in daily newspapers, and few of the papers sent critics. By the time the revue had moved downstairs to the main auditorium in November 1937 to begin a regular run, word of mouth had started to spread and critics did come. For the most part critics and patrons alike were pleased with what they saw. The *Times*'s backbencher who covered the opening called it "a revue out of the ordinary" and concluded "the left-wing theatre may take pride in this delayed descent from the usual soap box." Burns Mantle called it "bright with humorous sketches, lightly satirical in furthering labor's cause, adequately if not brilliantly played and surprisingly good entertainment." Richard Lockridge of the *Sun* took a middle ground, seeing it as a work by "class-conscious Leftists" all too often filled with "heavy-handed and dead-pan propaganda" but nonetheless possessing an "enlivening sting that has wit." He concluded its "appeal is not to the general audience." Some more conservative papers, either objecting to its politics or responding to its refusal to advertise, tried to ignore it and hoped it would go away. Others questioned whether militancy and lopsided political advocacy of any sort was a proper stance for a musical revue. Not surprisingly, the critic for the reactionary Chicago *Tribune*, reviewing the road company, saw it as "a sporadic victory for amateurism loaded with labor union propaganda." Yet certainly many of the better critics who had lambasted the equally left-wing *Parade* in 1935 came down squarely in *Pins and Needles*'s corner. From nearly a half-century's distance it is difficult to decide whether the critics had simply become inured to all the pinkish preaching and prosletyzing of the era, whether they themselves had undergone political conversions, or whether, in fact, the show did offer a more balanced outlook and a sunny disposition.

On the surface a semblance of balance could be seen in "The Little Red Schoolhouse," Emanuel Eisenberg's highly praised put-down of the left-wing soapbox dramas from which the *Times* said the revue had happily descended. When changes were made in 1939 they included "Papa Lewis, Mama Green," which made fun of the rivalry between the AFL and the CIO by turning the whole affair into a comic strip centering on a family quarrel. But all too many of the sketches and songs gratuitously injected slanted political muckraking into what could have been pleasant apolitical numbers. The show's hit tune cried "Sing Me a Song with Social Significance," and Rome and the sketch writers followed through with a vengeance. What might have been a high-stepping, escapist dance number became "Doin' the Reactionary" ("All the best dictators do it; Millionaires keep steppin' to it"), while a supposed love song, "One Big Union for Two," treated romance entirely in labor jargon such as "No scabbing when I'm out of town." Many of the skits flowed with a special venom. Marc Blitzstein, the best-known writer to contribute to the original version, slapped back at the Federal Theatre Project for its abandonment of his virulent *The Cradle Will Rock* by penning a sketch called "FTP Plowed Under."

As the long run rolled on, more new material, often reflecting the latest headlines, was added. After Munich, John Latouche and Arnold Horwitt contributed "Britannia Waives the Rules," and when two jazzed versions of *The Mikado* appeared on Broadway within days of each other, the show added its own cut-down version, "The Red Mikado," which lambasted the more stuffy conservative elements of society (such as the DAR, which had noisily banned Marion Anderson from using its facilities), and turned "Three Little Maids" into "Three little DAR's are we/ Full to the brim with bigotry." As had "Doin' the Reactionary," its Lord High Executioner's list of those who never would be missed coupled the vilest fascists with men such as Herbert Hoover and Neville Chamberlain, but found no room for the bloodiest communists.

Without seeing the show, especially without seeing it in its 1937 milieu, a theatrical historian might well wonder what so much of the hand-clapping was all about. At this remove it would seem that so unrelentingly supercharged an evening of political vitriol would be abrasively self-defeating. A point could have been better made by injecting a single protest song into a basically innocuous, mindless revue, where its contrast with the rest of the material would have brought home its message with particular cogency. Think, for example, of Ethel Waters delivering Irving Berlin's poignant "Supper Time," in the midst of *As Thousands Cheer*'s carefree humors. Moreover, Berlin got his message across simply by telling a story in song, and not by preaching or name-calling. Although Burns Mantle later recorded that *Pins and Needles* soon attracted "many rich loafers," one suspects that the most receptive playgoers, many of whom made repeat visits to the show, were those who were preconditioned to enjoy it. Fanatics of any ilk will often accept discomforts and tortures more balanced souls would unhesitatingly reject.

So it is not entirely surprising that *Pins and Needles* became a hit. What may at first seem surprising is the long run it achieved, playing for 1,108 performances or nearly three full years at a time when most hit shows were lucky to run six months. But the seemingly long run is deceptive. First of all, the Labor Stage sat fewer than three hundred patrons, about a fifth of what the average Broadway musical house holds. (The famed Princess Theatre shows all quickly moved away to larger theatres when they became successful.) The last part of its run was played at the slightly larger uptown Windsor Theatre, but it, too, was considerably smaller than even most playhouses devoted to non-musical attractions. Moreover, the show's running costs, without top-priced stars, with relatively small settings and no huge orchestra, allowed it to continue profitably at a figure that would have forced other revues to close.

Yet these disclaimers in no way detract from *Pins and Needles's* importance. For better or worse, depending on what one perceives as the purpose of theatre in general and of musical theatre specifically, the revue succeeded in achieving what *Parade* had tried and failed to do, namely, to impose a larger, more pervasive social or political conscience on the musical revue form. Heywood Broun blamed the reluctance of some critics to attend the show on an awareness of this, writing, "To put it bluntly, the reviewers believed that the girls who came from the machines might be less pulchritudinous than those whom Ziegfeld chose or even the dancers now selected by the Shuberts." Increasingly dominated, as it was to be, by artists of a pronounced liberal bent, the Broadway musical was soon to be incumbered by an obligation toward purposefulness that would take some of the wide-eyed fun out of song and dance entertainments.

The biggest revue hit among the three revues to premiere in 1938 took precisely the opposite tack. It was as if social injustices, political polarization, and the world's horrendous but obvious drift toward another war required extreme reactions. The I.L.G.W.U. showed one extreme, tackling the problems head on. Ole Olsen and Chic Johnson, two vaudeville and night-club clowns, showed the other, an escape into total zaniness. That their *Hellzapoppin* played in two large Broadway houses (including, eventually, the Winter Garden), yet ran far longer—1,404 performances—than even *Pins and Needles*, suggests the extreme most theatregoers preferred. Even ardent political advocates were frequently amused, suggesting the camaraderie of the philosopher and the pleasure-seeker.

What little method their madness demonstrated was that of a pair of audience-wise buffoons who knew that the purposeless pistol shots which kept punctuating the evening would suggest nothing of social unrest or international armaments races. Indeed, when Olsen was later asked to explain the show's success he noted, "I think it's because when times are so troubled and every time a person picks up a newspaper he feels like crying, people want good belly laughs."

The belly laughs began with a filmed prologue, a mock newsreel in which the attractions of the show were proclaimed by Hitler, with a marked Yiddish accent, Mussolini, whose Italian had a distinct Harlem drawl, and Roosevelt, who spoke gibberish. Then the stars arrived in a claptrap automobile, and the mayhem let loose in earnest. Supposed workmen trundled large ladders and other cumbersome work tools through rows of seats, requiring patrons to rise and back out of their way. On and off a lady appeared in one of the aisles searching for a man named Oscar. She made such a pest of herself that she was invited backstage, after which a shot was heard and Johnson emerged from the wings brandishing a bloody sword. Another well-dressed woman rose from her seat in the middle of a number and screamed, then ran out of the theatre shouting she had left her baby at the Automat. A man rode across the stage at intervals on an eight-foot unicycle, while at times a second man rolled across the stage in a straitjacket. A delivery boy walked up and down the aisles attempting to find the buyer of a plant. With each appearance he made, the plant grew noticeably larger, and at the end of the evening, as playgoers were leaving, he was standing in the lobby forlornly trying to deliver what had become a small tree. A score mostly by composer Sammy Fain and lyricist Charles Tobias got lost in the mayhem.

Not everybody in the first-night audience apparently knew what to make of such untoward bedlam, although most playgoers soon found themselves having fun. Critics were a different matter, the vast majority turning thumbs down on the evening. Many of those who did report that they found the show enjoyable still suggested it was too much of the same thing and eventually palled. For example, John Anderson of the *Journal-American* observed that the revue "starts out to be hilariously insane at the top of its voice and firmly yells itself into a messy bore."

One noteworthy exception to the nay-sayers was Walter Winchell. He was then probably the most widely read and influential of Broadway columnists as well as drama critic for the *Daily Mirror* and a hugely popular radio reporter. His morning-after review proclaimed "The slapstickiest, slaphappiest troupe of maniacs ever assembled on any stage is to be hilariously enjoyed." From then on his columns and his radio broadcasts regularly promoted the show, so much so, in fact, that he is generally conceded to have turned what might have been a failure or at best a minor success into a major hit.

In later years Olsen and Johnson offered similar entertainments: *Sons o' Fun* (1941), *Laffing Room Only* (1944), and *Pardon Our French* (1950). None of these later revues, except the last, was a failure, but their runs of 742, 232, and 100 performances respectively indicate that audiences quickly came to feel enough of such lunacy was enough.

Two nights after the premiere of *Hellzapoppin*, Max Gordon, George S. Kaufman, and Moss Hart relit the Music Box with *Sing Out the News*, a show which Stanley Green has labeled "the uptown sister of *Pins and Needles.*" Not only was its stance as staunchly liberal or leftist as the labor revue, but its songs were by that show's songwriter, Harold Rome; another alumnus, Charles Friedman, was credited with both direction and sketches, although Kaufman and Hart actually wrote much of the material. Perhaps because Kaufman and Hart were themselves successful and so understood that success was inherently neither evil nor corrupting, they imbued the whole show with a more even-handed, sunnier disposition than *Pins and Needles* usually had displayed. One of the drollest skits blended politics and Rodgers and Hart's *I Married an Angel.* In Kaufman and Hart's version Republican bigwigs despair of finding a candidate to oppose Roosevelt until an angel flies through their window. They pick him to head their ticket, only to discover he is sympathetic to the New Deal. Marshaling all their best arguments, they finally convert him to the Republican cause, whereupon his wings fall off. That some of the earlier bitterness remained could be seen in a sketch in which a youngster who tries to reconcile groups of rich and poor children is arrested for disturbing the peace. But even Rome's songs were sunnier and one, which in the show celebrated the birth of a black baby, swept the nation as "Franklin D. Roosevelt Jones," although its actual title was simply "F.D.R. Jones."

Once again critics and playgoers found themselves at odds. Notices were largely favorable, the sort that would normally assure a long run, but *Sing Our the News* struggled for fourteen weeks, then threw in the towel. Clearly, the great hordes of regular Broadway playgoers wanted their revues to be carefree and, probably, largely apolitical. Unlike their contemporaries behind the scenes, patrons still accepted the idea that a revue's purpose was, simply and unabashedly, to entertain.

The decade of the 1930s ended with a splurge of activity. Seven of 1939's fifteen musicals were revues. And what a mixed bag they were! The first to open was basically an American version of Noel Coward's London revue, *Words and Music*. Called *Set to Music* here, it starred Beatrice Lillie and allowed her to introduce "Mad About the Boy" and "I've Been to a Marvelous Party" to New York audiences. It ran only 129 performances.

Just over two weeks later *One for the Money* premiered. Originally a straw-hat revue, it came to New York with a cast of young unknowns, a stylish staging by John Murray Anderson with designs by Raoul Pène duBois, an unexceptional score by Morgan Lewis, and superior sketches and lyrics by Nancy Hamilton. Miss Hamilton's work looked steadfastly in a political direction opposite to that of *Pins and Needles* and *Sing Out the News*, but without the often heavy-handed militancy that had characterized those shows. It was, in effect, the right's genteel reply to the more raucous left. At one point the show sang, "We think that right is right and wrong is left." But playgoers, even the cushiest ones, were no more interested in this side of the political fence than they were in the other, at least in musical revues. So the show managed just a few performances more than had *Set to Music*. In the long run it was the revue's young cast that left its mark in the entertainment world, including Brenda Forbes, Ruth Matteson, Grace McDonald, Philip Bourneuf, Don Loper, Keenan Wynn, and, most of all, Gene Kelly and Alfred Drake. A pair of subsequent editions were called, as might be expected, *Two for the Show* (1940), and *Three To Make Ready* (1946). The former was no more successful than the first edition, but left behind

"How High the Moon"; the latter, by far the least political of the series, roamed broadly in its search for amusement and starred Ray Bolger. Not surprisingly it chalked up the longest run of the series—more than 300 performances.

The failed Federal Theatre Project production of *Sing for Your Supper*, another basically leftist entertainment, was the source for "Ballad for Americans," an extended musical piece by lyricist John Latouche and composer Earl Robinson, which was an uncommonly popular propaganda piece in World War II, and which as "The Ballad of Uncle Sam" had served as the musical's finale.

By far the biggest revue hit of the year was *The Streets of Paris*, a wild hodgepodge produced by the Shuberts in conjunction with Olsen and Johnson, and which starred Bobby Clark, Luella Gear, Carmen Miranda, Bud Abbott and Lou Costello, and featured in lesser assignments Jean Sablon, "Think a Drink" Hoffman, Gower Champion, and Ramon Vinay. Apart from replacing Bob Hope in the 1936 edition of the *Follies*, this was Clark's first solo appearance before a Broadway audience since the suicide of his partner, Paul McCullough. Clark and McCullough had delighted audiences since their Broadway debut in the second *Music Box Revue*, with the heftier, mustachioed Mc-Cullough, usually wrapped in a shaggy raccoon coat, serving as a babyish, whimpering foil to Clark's aggressive conniver. Their first appearance often involved a tussle to retrieve a discarded cigar, a tussle Clark always won. From the start Clark was recognized as the more dynamic of the pair. Now alone, Clark confirmed that he was one of the funniest and greatest of all Broadway clowns, albeit one of the most limited. For Clark was essentially a picture and an attitude. The picture was that of a shortish man dressed in clothes which had seen better days, brandishing a sawed-off cane and his retrieved cigar. His bright, mischievous eyes were framed in painted-on glasses. The attitude was a perpetual leer. His acrobatic ability—he could move with the lightning speed of a grasshopper—allowed the picture to be seen from all sides, and the leer never faded.

Clark's best moments in the new revue were a skit and a song. Playing opposite the acid Miss Gear in "The Convict's Return," he assumed all the male roles—a senile old man, a loyal retainer, an escaped convict, and a pursuing lawman. The guffaws came from Clark's increasingly frenetic attempts to make the requisite costume changes. The raunchy song, right up Clark's rather seedy alley, was "Robert the Roué (from Reading Pa.)." A lyric such as "I usually play in the hay— Hey!" might have been objectionable or simply stupid in other hands, but Clark's panache turned it into a belly laugh. Abbott and Costello, in their only Broadway appearance, used a mental institution, mistaken for a swank hotel, as the setting for some of their own lunacies. The evening's most popular song, "South American Way," was put over by the Brazilian Miss Miranda and Chilean Vinay. The show ran eight months, a relatively long stand at the time. One sign that an improving economic picture was helping at the box office was the raising of the show's top ticket from $3.30 to $4.40 once its success seemed assured.

Although "Are You Havin' Any Fun?" was another best-selling song of the day, its popularity could not propel *George White's Scandals* past a fifteen-week run. Atkinson noted that White had retained "the formula that served him in the gilded age" and that he had "assembled the usual virtues and vices in a swiftly paced revue." The critic then listed the virtues as "a chorus worth gaping at, a song or two that rises above mediocrity, a heat-treated dance called the Mexiconga." He also praised the cast, especially dancer Ann Miller, thereby acknowledging White's continuing emphasis on dancing. Two old *Scandals* veterans, Willie and Eugene Howard, led an excellent roster of comics that also included Ben Blue and The Three Stooges, but the show's comedy was seen as particularly weak and sometimes unnecessarily smutty. That in itself might not have been fatal, but Atkinson's review, with its falling back on words such as "formula" and "usual," and calling the twenties by a term customarily reserved for an era even longer gone, suggests that he may have been mirroring the reaction of many playgoers who could find some enjoyment in such entertainments all the while sensing they were a superannuated genre. That left open the question of what sort of revue, if any, could replace the old school.

The year's last revue, another graduate from the summer circuit, was called simply and appropriately *The Straw Hat Revue*. To the extent that it is remembered at all, it is recalled for its cast of rising young talents including Imogene Coca, Alfred Drake, Danny Kaye, and Jerome Robbins. But it, too, could not point out real new directions.

Nor could any of 1940's nine revues. The most successful was in one major respect a novelty, for, as its title announced, *It Happens on Ice* was performed almost entirely by skaters. It offered the beloved clown Joe Cook as star, complete with all his Rube Goldberg inventions; its score was by Vernon Duke, and its decor by Norman Bel Geddes. Essentially it was the sort of mindless spectacle that had once been the stock-in-trade of the Hippodrome, further down on Sixth Avenue, and more latterly was seen at the Radio City Music Hall, which was situated just to the north in the same Rockefeller Center where the ice show played. As far as the year's other revues went, they ranged from the old girlie-type with the last of the *Earl Carroll Vanities*—the edition with the infamous miking—through the single-star-centered vehicle that Ed Wynn had popularized in the 1920s and which he pulled off again with *Boys and Girls Together*, and the star-studded Shubert-style of the early and mid-thirties with *Keep Off the Grass* (the cast of this fiasco included Jimmy Durante, Ray Bolger, José Limon, Larry Adler, Jane Froman, and Ilka Chase), to any number of potpourris of the new-faces style the most successful of which were *Two for the Show* and *Meet the People*.

Although the ice spectacle started a decade-long series, it cannot be considered as part of the theatrical mainstream. So the rarely more than moderate successes of the other revues of the day proclaimed the malaise affecting the genre. No doubt the problem had been long in coming. As far back as 1929 sound films had begun to drain away the cream of Broadway talent, a drain aggravated by the onset of the Depression. The politicalization of many revues undoubtedly alienated other playgoers, as did, probably, the specialized brainlessness of Olsen and Johnson's variety. Moreover, in an ever-shrinking theatre, revues were seen to have little or no afterlife, thus depriving writers of additional income. Amateur groups, school groups, and even summer stock theatre preferred to revive book shows, which usually required less scenery and eye-filling choruses, and fewer particularly trained types such as dancers or uniquely gifted comedians. Increasingly, the better writers, especially younger ones, turned their efforts away from revue to musical comedy and operetta.

In 1941 only two revues reached Broadway, one in January and one in December. *Crazy with the Heat* was short-lived, while *Sons o' Fun* ran nearly two years, thanks to Olsen and Johnson's loyal fans. In the next year, however, matters began to turn around, so that from 1942 through 1948 Broadway was to see a number of superb revues, which, as time would show, were to represent the last gasp of the genre's oldest traditions.

8

The Faltering Forties

The 1930s saw the Depression, its consequent political turmoil, and the flourishing of both sound films and radio all take their toll on the nature and popularity of the revue as a theatrical genre. They took their toll in different ways. Hard times cost playhouses audiences, and to some extent made money sometimes more difficult to come by for producing shows, even if, as we have seen, many of our greatest revues were produced in the Depression and enjoyed reasonably long runs. The draining away of talent, especially young talent, may have been more critical, although here a number of remarkable older writers and performers who remained loyal to Broadway helped obscure the problem for a decade or more. Inevitably the political polarization faded with coming of prosperity and did not return until the economic and social upheavals of the 1960s, by which time the traditional revue was all but dead. Of course, every aspect of theatre was affected by these developments. Allowing for inevitable evolution, matters might have returned to "normal," but for two developments in the 1940s.

The first of these was America's entry into World War II, which suddenly and dramatically exacerbated the drain of younger talent. In the long run the war would also create a markedly changed social and intellectual climate that would have serious repercussions for our stages. That, however, was not immediately apparent. But in the short run, the very service that most commandingly pulled away young players helped give them back in one of the most memorable of all American revues, *This Is the Army.*

At heart the show was a huge, stirring, patriotic spectacle, the distant offspring, in a small sense, of such "oratorical" entertainment as the 1781 *Temple of Minerva.* But playgoers did not have to reach so far back for an antecedent. World War I had seen a very similar show. It had been called *Yip, Yip, Yaphank,* after a famous Long Island army camp, and it had been the brainchild of the same man who created *This Is the Army,* Irving Berlin. Indeed, Berlin underscored the connection between these two all-soldier revues by resurrecting two famous songs from the earlier production, "Mandy," which Ziegfeld had afterwards appropriated for his 1919 *Follies,* and the second most popular of all American World War I songs, "Oh, How I Hate To Get Up in the Morning," which Berlin himself had sung in the original and which he sang again in the new revue. There were other parallels, not so patently discernible. Marian Spitzer, who among her myriad talents was a theatrical historian, recorded the comparisons in an article for the *Times* shortly after *This Is the Army* opened. She showed how similar scenes and similar musical numbers were positioned in comparable slots in both shows. Thus, in *Yaphank* a "Follies" number with soldiers in drag as Marilyn Miller, Ann Pennington, and other stage ladies of the day gave way to a Stage Door Canteen number in *This Is the Army,* with soldiers in drag as Vera Zorina, Gypsy Rose Lee, and their contemporaries. Both shows ended with the cast marching off, in 1918 to fight the war to end all wars, in 1942 to make certain "this time is the last time." Both shows had little in the way of dialogue or sketches, of which none was memorable. In the case of *This Is the Army* a decision to play exceptionally large auditoriums on tour probably influenced the minimizing of dialogue, although soldiers at one point did exchange tall tales. In another "skit" a soldier turned his spell at KP into a potato juggling routine. But if they sacrificed the spoken word, both shows had superior scores, and therein lay a major distinction.

As we have said, Berlin was, along with Arthur Schwartz, our most successful composer for revues. More than a composer, as his own lyricist he was capable of adding words to his melodies that were especially befitting to revue requirements. Although his score for *Yip, Yip, Yaphank* could not compare with those he would shortly create for some *Follies*, his *Music Box Revues* and for *As Thousands Cheer*, it was several notches above those that had typified virtually all earlier revues. Moreover, it appeared just as revues were coming into the height of popularity and were often to be filled with fresh, memorable songs. By contrast, Berlin's far greater score for *This Is the Army* can in retrospect be seen as the last great revue score, with only Schwartz's melodies for *Inside U.S.A.* in serious contention for the honor. Curiously, at the time of its premiere the score was perceived differently. Broadway in general and Berlin in particular had been in a creative slump for several seasons. Great Broadway scores had been few and far between. Most critics instantly recognized the excellence of Berlin's new score and hoped it signalled a turn-around. In fact, it did. But not in any way that might have been foretold and certainly not for the musical revue.

This Is the Army's two biggest hits were its rousing yet humorous title song (technically, "This Is the Army, Mr. Jones") and its best love ballad, the plaintive "I Left My Heart at the Stage Door Canteen." Both songs were ragingly popular and exemplified the deceptive simplicity and directness that so often characterized the songwriter. But there were many other superb songs, several of which enjoyed some popularity during the period. "I'm Getting Tired So I Can Sleep" was another bittersweet ballad. The Air Force was saluted in the high-flying "American Eagles" and in a thumping number that combined a fight song and a love song, "With My Head in the Clouds." "That's What the Well-Dressed Man in Harlem Will Wear" caught the jivey black idioms of the day. There was, indeed, scarcely a weak number in the whole show. Because the lyrics, even of the love songs, were so extremely topical, filled with army jargon and references to military con-

The second act "ballet" in the 1894 *Passing Show*. See page 20 for details and critical reactions. (*Theatre Collection, Museum of the City of New York*)

The scene in which Caruso's trial for pinching a lady was spoofed in *The Follies of 1907*. *(Theatre Collection, Museum of the City of New York)*

A scene from *The Passing Show of 1914*. Note the feeling of a vaudeville sketch done "in one." The "lady" in the middle is George W. Monroe. *(Theatre Collection, Museum of the City of New York)*

A Ben Ali Haggin tableau from *The Ziegfeld Follies of 1919*.
(Theatre Collection, Museum of the City of New York)

Florenz Ziegfeld. *(Theatre Collection, Museum of the City of New York)*

Tillie Losch, Fred and Adele Astaire, Frank Morgan, and Helen Broderick in *The Band Wagon*. *(The Billy Rose Collection of The New York Public Library at Lincoln Center)*

Howard Dietz and Arthur Schwartz. *(Theatre Collection, Museum of the City of New York)*

Marilyn Miller and Clifton Webb pretending they are Joan Crawford and Douglas Fairbanks, Jr., in *As Thousands Cheer*. *(Theatre Collection, Museum of the City of New York)*

The "Four Little Angels of Peace" number from *Pins and Needles*.
(Theatre Collection, Museum of the City of New York)

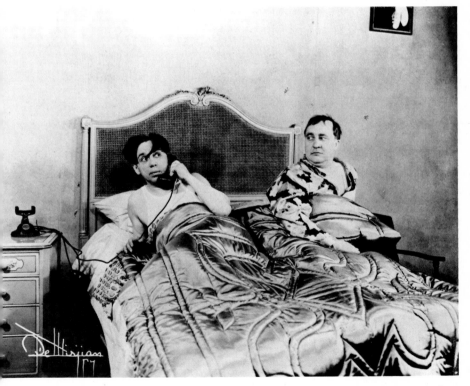

Olsen and Johnson in an intimate, romantic moment from *Hellzapoppin*.
(Theatre Collection, Museum of the City of New York)

A scene from *Lend an Ear*'s send-up of 1920s' musicals, "The Gladiola Girl." The petite, sedate chorus girl on the far right is Carol Channing. *(Theatre Collection, Museum of the City of New York)*

Ann Miller and Mickey Rooney in a publicity shot for *Sugar Babies*.
(Theatre Collection, Museum of the City of New York)

Irving Berlin singing "Oh, How I Hate To Get Up in the Morning" in *This Is the Army*. *(Theatre Collection, Museum of the City of New York)*

Bert Williams. *(Theatre Collection, Museum of the City of New York)*

Bert Lahr. *(Theatre Collection, Museum of the City of New York)*

Beatrice Lillie. *(Theatre Collection, Museum of the City of New York)*

cerns, the songs are now rarely heard. But this in no way lessens their excellence.

For contemporary playgoers the songs were put across in a magnificent spectacle that began with a cast of three hundred uniformed men (including Pvt. Burl Ives, Pvt. Anthony Ross, Pvt. Julie Oshins, Pvt. Gary Merrill, and radio's broken-voiced Henry Aldrich, Staff Sgt. Ezra Stone, who also staged the show) arranged in banked rows for a "Military Minstrel Show," went on to have pilots standing on the wing of a huge plane, and concluded with the troops marching out through the audience. Especially in the high-tensioned atmosphere of 1942 it was a singularly exciting evening in the theatre. Miss Spitzer, who as a young girl had thought *Yip, Yip, Yaphank* provided a once-in-a-lifetime thrill, concluded, "It happened twice in a lifetime."

Only time would reveal that the excitement did not presage a return to renewed vigor for the revue but rather that it was the sort of feverish outburst of creativity known to precede—at least in drama and novels—a final collapse.

For 1942 audiences, not possessed of crystal balls, the year must have seemed a busy and largely undistinguished one. Whereas two revues had raised their curtains the preceding year, over a dozen appeared in the first war year. Sticklers might balk at the count, for more than half represented a curious departure from expected norms. In essence they were more vaudeville than revue. Although they were initiated by one man, a minor night-club operator named Clifford C. Fischer, they responded to several requirements of the moment. First of all, the war had brought on the long-sought prosperity, meaning there was a better chance to keep all of Broadway's surviving theatres lit than there had been in a decade. Second, with so many young creative and performing talents off fighting the war, older men, younger men who had been rejected for one reason or another, and women of all ages would have to comprise the cast and, where possible, provide their own material. Vaudeville and vaudevillians, with some night-club performers thrown in for good measure, were clearly the answer. Moreover, since vaudeville shows required less scenery than book musicals or most revues, they could be mounted cheaply and quickly. The shows had such titles as *Priorities of 1942, Keep 'Em Laughing, Harlem Cavalcade, Top-Notchers, New Priorities,* and *Show Time,* and they offered such notable performers as Willie Howard, Victor Moore, William Gaxton, Paul and Grace Hartman, Noble Sissle, Flournoy Miller, George Jessel, Jack Haley, Hazel Scott, Ella Logan, and young Zero Mostel. Ed Wynn produced and starred in his own vaudeville-revue, *Laugh, Town, Laugh.* They met with varying degrees of success, but by the end of the year their novelty had worn away and the rash of vaudeville-like productions ended as suddenly as it had begun.

Nostalgia may also have played a part in the success of some of these hastily assembled olios. With the fearful defeats that beset us early in the war and the uncertain future that awaited us, old, familiar faces, often cavorting through old, familiar routines must have provided hours of comforting escape. Nostalgia and the appeal of another largely passé type of theatre may have occasioned the production of a revue that opened after several of the vaudevilles had appeared and just a few nights before the premiere of *This Is the Army. Star and Garter* was, as its name suggested, a resucitation of the very cheap thrill burlesque that New York's feisty Mayor LaGuardia had shuttered only a few seasons before. Of course, it was "glorified" burlesque, produced by Mike Todd at an expense and with a stylish flair alien to the Minskys and their competitors. One of its stars was Gypsy Rose Lee, by far the classiest, most savvy graduate of the old Minsky school. Georgia Sothern, considered by many her leading rival, appeared in support. Its other star was Bobby Clark, whose leering way with broad comedy so perfectly suited the show and whose very presence was a tribute to the many great, unheralded roustabouts who had spelled the strippers in modern burlesque's heyday. Much of the material was old hat, but workable. And while Irving Berlin, Harold Rome, and Harold Arlen were all listed in the musical credits their contributions were not top drawer. All in all it was good, dirty fun, propelled into a long run by the resurgent economic situation. So successful was the show that the Shuberts brought out their own burlesque-inspired revue before the year's end, *Wine, Women and Song.* Anything other producers could do, the Shuberts could do more tackily. Margie Hart was not Gypsy

Rose Lee, and Jimmy Savo, for all his endearing skills, no Bobby Clark. Still, at two shows a day, the musical did run sixteen weeks.

Two other more traditional revues, *Of V We Sing* and *Let Freedom Sing*, relied heavily on unknowns and on patriotic sentiment. Both failed, as did the year's last revue, a 1942 edition of *New Faces*.

In theatrical terms, *This Is the Army* was an early entrant in the 1942–43 season, the same season that altered for decades to come the nature and slant of the American musical theatre. For late in that season *Oklahoma!* opened. And with it came the second development of the 1940s to affect the revue.

During the seasons preceding *Oklahoma!*'s premiere our lyric stage had drifted in the doldrums. True, the early 1940s had seen the arrival of such daring, superior shows as *Cabin in the Sky*, *Pal Joey*, and *Lady in the Dark*. Yet for all their success they seemed, at least at the time, to have led nowhere and to have established no real precedents. For the most part Broadway musical comedies were slick, flashy, brassy affairs with their real merit to be found in their basic theatrical know-how, their superb productions, and the performances and allure of their stars. Cole Porter, for example, had enjoyed a series of hits, but his scores for *DuBarry Was a Lady*, *Panama Hattie*, *Let's Face It!*, and *Something for the Boys* were seen as indicative of a declining creativity, and without such talents as Ethel Merman, Bert Lahr, and Danny Kaye these shows might well have been failures. Berlin's *Louisiana Purchase*, despite a few superior ballads, needed an all-star cast to keep it before the footlights.

Operetta was in an even worse way. With the rise of identifiably American talents in the teens and 1920s—Jerome Kern and more especially George Gershwin, Cole Porter, and Vincent Youmans—operetta had begun to fall into disrepute as something alien and absurd. Of course, Kern, with Oscar Hammerstein II, had demonstrated in *Show Boat* how totally and brilliantly operetta could be Americanized, and Kern, first with Otto Harbach and then again with Hammerstein, also had shown in *The Cat and the Fiddle* and *Music in the Air* how an amalgam of European and American styles could be achieved. But however successful these works were they spawned no equally successful progeny. *Show Boat*, especially, stood for years an isolated beacon. The rise of Nazi Germany and the outbreak of World War II exacerbated the problems for operetta in that it was perceived, however incorrectly, to be a basically Germanic genre.

The musical revue had fared only a little better, becoming less memorably musical and seeming even to lose much of its wit, bite, and panache. Stumbling along in this weakened condition, it was scarcely prepared for the knockdown punch that *Oklahoma!* unwittingly administered.

Singlehandedly *Oklahoma!* revived the failing fortunes of both book shows in general and operetta in particular. Its solid book and superb melodies and lyrics were meshed with magnificent ballets to take up where *Show Boat* had pioneered over fifteen years before in creating a new American operetta form. Before long new American operettas—although they were now called musical plays—and American musical comedies were tripping over each other to announce how artistically they had integrated song, story, and dance, how they had dispensed with cardboard lovers to present instead three-dimensional people who faced problems fraught with social significance.

The new meaningfulness of the musical theatre reflected to some extent the maturing of the militant left-wing political posturing that had sometimes bedeviled the theatre of the 1930s. It replaced the earlier stridency and belligerency with a more sober, if no less determined liberalism. Yet while the show-wise liberals who wrote many of the most glorious musicals of the 1940s, 1950s, and early 1960s achieved many of their aims, they often, by masking their philosophies in treacliness and preachiness, took much of the old brainless fun out of the musical theatre. Artistically, there was little inherent reason why they should not have found the revue a lively, potent forum for their stands. Yet the fact remains that the new order of book musicals became so much the rage that virtually no major talent, especially none of the older established talents, ever returned to it. Of course, the awareness that book musicals had longer money-making lives after Broadway may have been a significant goad to those who advocated redistributing the wealth and redirecting the social system all the while, as some noted chucklingly, they wrote from their magnificent homes and apartments. Even so, the revue was not yet down for the final count. The night after *Oklahoma!*'s premiere, and, of course, long before its influence could be felt or even imagined, the *Ziegfeld Follies of 1943* came to town. The show was to run over 500 performances, far more than any of Ziegfeld's own editions had achieved, but its success could be attributed as much to wartime prosperity and to a certain nostalgia for a legendary series as to any real excellences. The Shuberts, who had covertly produced the two editions of the mid-1930s, this time openly acknowledged their sponsorship. The acknowledgment was not all that necessary. The tackiness was tell-tale. Missing from the morning-after notices were the ecstatic, awed exclamations that had so regularly greeted Urban's designs and, to a smaller extent, Minnelli's later ones. The critics who praised the settings and costumes did so with a perfunctory resignation. Those who felt obliged to report on their disappointment did so with more feeling. For example, Burton Rascoe of the *World-Telegram* bewailed that the scenery looked "as though it came from Cain's storehouse without much retouching." Milton Berle, who was later to become television's first major star, glamorous Ilona Massey and the perennial butler, Arthur Treacher, both of films, headed a cast that featured comedienne Sue Ryan and dancer-choreographer Jack Cole. All were excellent performers, but none, with the possible exception of Berle, were of a caliber equal to the old *Follies* stars. Ray Henderson, separated from his *Scandals'* partners, DeSylva and Brown, created the melodies that demonstrated a sad decline in his once surefire gifts. Oddly, the show was at its best where the old *Follies* had often been their weakest, in the dancing. But with Cole as choreographer the dances were more imaginatively balletic than had been customary. His jitterbug-influenced "Wedding of the Solid Sender" and his more exotic "Hindu Serenade" were among the evening's highlights. That such dances were highlights was a small hint of things to come in American revue, although it could not be foreseen at the time.

The huge success of the revival may have prompted two subsequent 1943 revivals of dormant but once popular revues. Both revivals proved short-lived. The first was *Chauve-Souris of 1943*. Try as it might it could not recapture the charm of the original. The second was *Artists and Models*, with which the Shuberts had once hoped to compete with Earl Carroll. This time, however, night-club owner Lou Walters was listed as producer, and the show he offered was a mediocre mélange of vaudeville, burlesque, and traditional revue.

Laugh Time, a vaudeville on the order of those produced the year before, enjoyed an extended run with Ethel Waters and Frank Fay heading the cast, while *Bright Lights of 1944*, which opened and closed in one week in 1943, resorted to the long-discarded idea of a thin plot to hold together its songs and sketches. In it, two vaudeville favorites, Smith and Dale, portrayed a pair of old two-a-day artists, now reduced to waiting on tables, who decide to produce a show.

An unsuspected glimpse of the future was offered to playgoers when concert impresario Sol Hurok presented Katherine Dunham and her exciting company of black dancers in *A Tropical Revue*, a sizzling evening of rhythmic black dances culled from various times and places —harking back to the "Darktown Strutters' Ball" and flying down almost to a contemporary Rio for "Bahiana." Gone were the oldtime style skits depicting Rastus in Jimtown. Even an occasional lyric seemed unimportant. The evening was musical and choreographic from beginning to end. A surprise hit, the show later toured and returned the following season.

That following season needed all the help it could get—at least as far as revues were concerned. The ghost of Ziegfeld hovered over what promised to be its most glamorous revue. Billy Rose, who had delusions of Ziegfeldian grandeur, had purchased the magnificent Ziegfeld Theatre, which for a decade had served as a grind film house, and had lovingly and noisily restored it to the legitimate fold. When he found that much of the backstage apparatus at the house had been removed he purchased materials from the old Apollo, which had long been home to the *Follies'* rival, the *Scandals*. He saw to it that really meaningless coincidence also received a loud trumpeting. He called his revue *Seven Lively Arts*, and on paper he enlisted an awesome, seemingly foolproof roster of writers and performers—Cole Porter and Igor Stravinsky for the music, Moss Hart, George S. Kaufman, Ben Hecht, and others for the skits, and Beatrice Lillie, Bert Lahr, Doc Rockwell, Albert Carroll, Benny Goodman, Alicia Markova, and Anton Dolin to bring the music and comedy to life. Unfortunately, nothing is foolproof on Broadway. Only a huge advance sale prevented the show from being a short-lived bomb. The show's "artiest" moments, such as the Stravinsky ballet, were dismissed by highbrows as trite and by regular playgoers as pretentious; most of the comedy fell flat, and Porter's score, except for the plaintive ballad "Ev'ry Time We Say Goodbye," left behind nothing memorable. Even Norman Bel Geddes's lavish sets—as lavish as certain wartime shortages permitted—compared unfavorably with the sumptuous wonders of yesteryear.

Brushing aside two more vaudeville-revues, *Take a Bow*, which had closed the 1943–44 season, and *Star Time*, which had appeared early in the 1944–45 season, the only other revues in 1944 were a pair that followed on the heels of *Seven Lively Arts*. *Laughing Room Only* was the third in Olsen and Johnson's madcap series. It ran six months, a far shorter run than either of its predecessors, suggesting enough was enough. However, it did have the only really popular song to emerge from these zany mayhems, a cornball ditty, "Feudin' and Fightin'." *Sing Out, Sweet Land!* was billed as a "Salute to American Folk and Popular Music," thus, along with *A Tropical Revue*, it moved away from traditional revue material to emphasize music, and older, generally fondly remembered music at that. Despite a fine Theatre Guild production, headed by Alfred Drake and Burl Ives, the entertainment proved too esoteric for the tired businessman.

But for the appearance of yet two more of the variety show-cum-revues, the black *Blue Holiday* and *Concert Varieties* (rushed in to fill the stage left empty by the failure of *Seven Lively Arts*), 1945 might have gone down in the records as the first year since virtually the beginning of the century without a single new revue! Only four appeared in 1946. Two were negligible: *Tidbits of 1946* and another black choreographic showpiece, *Bal Negre*; the other two enjoyed long runs. *Three To Make Ready* proved to be the last in the series that had started with *One for the Money*. Unlike its predecessors, it shied away from a rightist slant, perhaps sensing that, while later that year voters would respond to the Republican campaign slogan "Had Enough?" with a loud "yes," the more ardent politicalization of the revue had run its course. Still, its most appealing moment, with Ray Bolger affectionately re-creating "The Old Soft Shoe," implicitly suggested progress was not always for the better. When Bolger was not on stage the revue seemed very ordinary indeed. By contrast, *Call Me Mister*, offering a cast filled with war veterans and dedicated largely to commenting on the problems, admittedly often comic, of their return to civilian life, did have a certain political commitment, a rather easygoing liberalism. The evening's most moving sequence had the ex-soldiers reverently remembering their recently dead commander-in-chief in "The Face on the Dime." But there was nothing political about the revue's hilarious show-stopper, a send-up of the raging craze for Latin dances, "South America, Take It Away!" It was sung by the production's leading lady, Betty Garrett.

For all their success, *Three To Make Ready* and *Call Me Mister* could not hide the fact that the revue as a genre was a passing theatrical form. Nor did 1947 present any cogent reasons to reassess this conclusion. Its three offerings arrived late in the year, and the first two were short-lived. Only Edith Piaf's reputation helped her untitled Continental vaudeville chalk up a month's run, while a Dunhamless black dance show, *Caribbean Carnival*, folded after a week and a half. The year's lone hit was a sleeper and an oddity. *Angel in the Wings* was a small-scaled, low-budget entertainment devised largely as a vehicle for the Hartmans, a team of droll dancers who heretofore had made a career in vaudeville, night clubs, and, occasionally, in films. Wisely, the revue was presented in one of Broadway's smallest theatres so that these choreographic farceurs could quickly establish an intimate rapport with their audiences. Homely Paul, usually meandering dazed and baffled, made the perfect foil for the pert, self-assured, attractive Grace. They regaled playgoers with their spoofs of native dancing, cooking classes, and garden parties. When they themselves were in the wings changing, moonfaced Hank Ladd provided comic monologues and ditties, and young Elaine Stritch brought down the house with her paean to simple jungle living, "Civilization."

Matters took a sudden and surprising turn for the better in 1948. It was, indeed, something of an *annus mirabilis*. To an eternally optimistic segment of Broadway pundits it seemed a new day was about to dawn for the revue. Such optimism was rash. The truth was that 1948 would be put down as the last great year for the genre, and then even the best of the shows would be flawed. On the other hand, especially after making allowances for the shrunken nature of all live theatre, there was gratifyingly much to cheer about. The year's wonders might be, as one revue title modestly suggested, small, but wonders they were.

Because *Make Mine Manhattan* premiered in mid-January, little over a month after *Angel in the Wings*, and because it meant that the last four new musicals to reach Broadway had all been revues of one sort or another, fans and advocates of the form began a year-long rush into print with roseate predictions. Actually, *Make Mine Manhattan* was about on a par with *Angel in the Wings*, although a slicker, more patently costly production may have made it seem superior. Like the Hartman vehicle, it was a good, possibly a very good revue, but not a truly great one. If the sets and costumes had great immediate eye appeal, the songs were less popular (though sometimes more artful). A pronouncedly rhythmic hoe-down, "Saturday Night in Central Park," brought the first act to a rousing close but never approached the popularity of "Civilization" (which admittedly had been inserted into *Angel in the Wings* after the song had become widely sung on radio). Both revues excelled at comedy, although the Hartman show had a gentler thrust while the kidding of the later revue was less subtle in its special appeal to New Yorkers. *Make Mine Manhattan* is undoubtedly best recalled as the entertainment that catapulted young Sid Caesar to fame. Although its roster offered such other superb comics as Joshua Shelley and David Burns, Caesar wangled virtually all the biggest laughs in the skits. He was unforgettable as the pompous, egomaniacal Hollywood producer, come to make a film in New York, where he assured the Mayor that after the film was released New York City would be world-famous. Burns abetted him as the blasé, sarcastic onlooker. Shelley was given the two best comic songs. The first described the plight of a young lover who lives at the opposite end of the subway system from his girl. The second devastated the Stouffer-Schrafft school of tearoom, where you can eat all night without affecting your appetite. Hassard Short, who had lent his talents to the *Seven Lively Arts* debacle, mounted the work.

What promised to be an even bigger and better revue, *Inside U.S.A.*, raised its curtain in April. Schwartz and Dietz created the songs, while Moss Hart led the list of sketch writers. Bea Lillie and Jack Haley headed the cast, with dancer Valerie Bettis, handsome, strong-voiced John Tyers, and monologuist Herb Shriner in support. A strike in the recording industry had forced the performers to record the songs before the show went into rehearsal, so that playgoers were able to listen to them in the comfort of their living rooms before they saw and heard them in the theatre. Somehow, what sounded so clever and memorable on the phonograph didn't project effectively in vaster auditoriums. In fact, one of the funniest numbers, with Miss Lillie spoofing the old Jolson type of Dixie anthem, was cut before the show reached New York. Only "Haunted Heart" made its way into the Schwartz-Dietz canon, although several of the lighter songs such as "Rhode Island Is Famous for You" and "First Prize at the Fair" deserved a better fate. Nor was the comedy all that good.

Hilarities, another glorified vaudeville, arrived early in September, failed to live up to its title, and departed in less than two weeks. It was followed in short order by *Small Wonder*, an intimate revue with a superior cast and some superb moments, but which, in the expression of a later day, could not quite get it all together. If its score was weak and left Jack Cassidy and Joan Diener stranded, its comic potential in the hands of Tom Ewell, Mary McCarty, and Alice Pearce was often realized. Best of all was Miss McCarty's salute to bygone flappers in "Flaming Youth." Some theatre-folk suggested at the time that its then high price of $6 discouraged playgoers. Others felt that interest in all but the very best revues had evaporated. Whatever the reason, *Small Wonder* had a somewhat forced run of only four months.

As if saving the best for last, the year closed out with a smash-hit revue, *Lend an Ear*. Visually the show was unexceptional. Costumes and sets were tasteful, but no one gasped in awe as each new scene was revealed. Musically the evening was mediocre, with no song enjoying even the limited acclaim of "Saturday Night in Central Park" or "Haunted Heart." Yet none of this mattered, since the comedy and comedians were devastatingly hilarious and unforgettable. One comedienne in particular grabbed the spotlight whenever she so much as shuffled or barged or strided or minced or Charlestoned across the stage. She was a huge young lady with two giant spotlights of her own for eyes and with a voice that out-Chaliapined Chaliapin's basso and out-squealed Betty Boop. Playgoers who scurried to their programs to learn her name found she was Carol Channing. The name had a curious staid dignity to it, which her every movement and utterance disavowed. There seemed to be no end to her comic gifts. She could be a celebrity dutifully attempting to live up to every contradictory item gossip columnists wrote about her, or an opera singer endeavoring to do an opera without any music, or, best of all, a wildly energetic flapper chorus girl in a 1920s' musical comedy.

That last skit, "The Gladiola Girl," was more than an uproarious, right-on-the-mark spoof of the vivacious, melodic but inane confections of long bygone decades, it was one of the landmark masterpieces in the entire history of the American revue. A compère came before the curtain to announce that way back in 1926 "The Gladiola Girl" had been one of Broadway's biggest musical comedy hits and, in the practice of the time, had sent out numerous road companies, all but one of which eventually returned to New York. Now the missing road company had been located and looked as young and fresh as ever. Thus, 1948 New Yorkers could see the long-forgotten hit in all its pristine glory. Its story was simple and not all that original: boy meets girl, boy loses girl, boy gets girl. In this instance both boy and girl were very ordinary youngsters pretending to riches and importance not really theirs. (Sociologists might see something in the fact that the later English spoof of 1920s' musicals, *The Boy Friend*, reversed the situation and rich youngsters disclaimed their wealth and position.) Accompanying the fluffy story were equally fluffy songs. The gay party songs of the period's musicals were reflected in "Join Us in a Cup of Tea" and "A Little Game of Tennis." The inevitable love-nest song cropped up with "In Our Teeny Little Weeny Nest" (for two, naturally). Songs of expectant love and troth-plighting were mirrored in "Where Is the She for Me?" and "I'll Be True to You." And the rousing, shake-a-leg dance number was resurrected with great vim and vigor in "Doin' the Old Yahoo Step." The parody could not have appeared at a better moment, answering some need in the period's *Zeitgeist* far more successfully than *Small Wonder*'s "Flaming Youth." By the very next year Miss Channing would be the star of *Gentlemen Prefer Blondes* and a reassessment of the era of wonderful nonsense would be under way.

Several other bits managed to pull off intriguing blends of attitudes. "Friday Dancing Class" combined a sentimental look at children's dancing lessons with an affectionate yet amused commentary on the genteel tortures of such sessions, while "Santo Domingo," starting out as just another of the era's many south-of-the-border choreographic exhibitions, soon became a barbed treatise on the squalor and corruption behind the idyllic tropical palms.

Assisting Miss Channing were the brassy, beautiful Yvonne Adair, the pleasant leading man from films, William Eythe, tiny, dour George Hall, and an excellent dancer, Gene Nelson, who led the steppers in Gower Champion's routines.

On the face of it Broadway and aficionados of revue had cause to cheer, but sadly appearances were deceiving. The next two dozen or so years were to bring in a handful of memorable revues. Yet with each passing season it became increasingly obvious that something was wrong. Either we could no longer create superior revues or the public would not buy them. Something would have to be found, a new approach, a new style, a new format, if revues were to maintain a foothold in theatrical listings. Certainly Broadway would not give up without a good try. But what Broadway could not or would not recognize was that revue had lost its sense of balance and, sometimes, its sense of purpose.

9

New Visions

Just possibly, the jubilant hopes which 1948 kindled for a rebirth of the revue might have been realized but for the most important development in the entertainment field since the advent of sound films and the disheartening economics of the Depression fifteen or twenty years before. Of course at the outset only a handful of the more affluent could afford television sets, and those sets they did purchase and around which they began to gather a nightly coterie of friends presented rather primitive productions on screens that by only slightly later standards were ludicrously small. However, within two or three seasons sets became commonplace—especially in the homes of the very middle class that constituted the bulk of playgoers. Screens grew larger and larger. Productions waxed more ambitious and elaborate and began to enlist stars or to make important new names. Television's first big star was Milton Berle, the star of the last major *Ziegfeld Follies.* Soon Sid Caesar, so recently of *Make Mine Manhattan,* and Imogene Coca, from a more remote *New Faces,* became darlings of what desperate detractors referred to as the "boob tube." Their shows were essentially revues. Broadway columnist Ed Sullivan jumped on the bandwagon to offer almost pure vaudeville in black and white, two-dimensional terms. Needing new material every week for these young TV giants and their lesser copycats, the new form started to gobble up—and sometimes burn out—talent at an alarming rate. Even in its heyday Broadway never expected its best writers to create more than two or three shows a season. In the thirties Hollywood seemed more gluttonous and omnivorous. But nothing compared with the devastatingly greedy requirements of television. And given the salaries television offered, it was all but impossible for Broadway's revue writers and performers to resist. With a few notable exceptions, the best revues to appear over the following decade or so were to be the work of some important but aging loyalists (or very new comers)—though never again of major older composers.

Almost inevitably, 1949 was a letdown, and the year's very first revue exemplified the disappointment. Its title, *Along Fifth Avenue*, suggested it might have been aiming to be another *Make Mine Manhattan*. On paper its roster of performers looked even better than that of the earlier show. Heading the cast were two great clowns: Nancy Walker and Jackie Gleason. Walker was a tiny, dour-faced comedienne whose very presence wreaked havoc on her surroundings and, with side-splitting hilarity, on her. One critic said she could not strike an attitude without the attitude striking back. Heretofore she had appeared only in book shows. Gleason was a balloonish, pugnacious wiseguy whose best-laid plans went aft agley. In comic support were Hank Ladd and an as yet unrecognized George S. Irving. Two fine singers, Carol Bruce and Donald Richards, were called on for the romantic musical numbers. But none of these superior performers could fully overcome the lack-luster songs and sketches. The show's best moment was a comic song, "If This Is Glamour," with which Miss Walker vented her spleen on fashion trend setters. A few decades earlier, when Broadway had been larger and healthier economically, even a second-rate revue such as this might have found a comfortable niche. As it was, the show ran five months, although it wound up in the red. Competing for Broadway's increasingly limited patronage was simply too much against such hits as *Where's Charley?*; *Lend An Ear*; *Kiss Me, Kate*; and, eventually,

South Pacific. Significantly, both stars were to spend some of their best years regaling television audiences.

The Hartmans, abandoning the intimacy that had made *Angel in the Wings* so effective, came a cropper in a gargantuan hodgepodge, *All for Love,* while Ken Murray had even less luck with *Blackouts.* The show had run for years and years in Hollywood, which was probably enough to set New York's chauvinistic critics against it in any case. But it was also a mediocre entertainment, sometimes mushy, sometimes raunchy, always bathetic.

The year's last revue was its best, but not really good enough considering the times. *Touch and Go* was largely the work of two very remarkable young talents, Walter and Jean Kerr, with music by Jay Gorney of "Brother, Can You Spare a Dime?" fame. Gorney provided several commendable ballads—"It Will Be All Right (in a Hundred Years)," and "This Had Better Be Love," but it was the Kerrs' comic moments that made the evening sparkle. They had uproarious fun with a musical *Hamlet* as Rodgers and Hammerstein might have done it ("You're a Queer One, Dear Ophelia") and a version of Cinderella à la Tennessee Williams. A highlight was a comic song, "Be a Mess," which spoofed the harried heroines who had recently won Academy Awards for their portrayers. Yet its very many bright spots could not help the revue run any longer than had *Along Fifth Avenue.*

Both the revues which opened early in 1950 had assets to recommend them, but not sufficient goodies to really succeed. *Alive and Kicking* offered David Burns and Jack Gilford in some better comic moments and excellent choreography by Jack Cole, while *Dance Me a Song* discovered a shy, droll monologuist in Wally Cox. In the spring, *Tickets, Please* opened with Grace Hartman announcing that if critics were themselves criticized they would be too embarrassed to pan the show, so she and husband Paul promptly gave the aisle-sitters a Bronx cheer. Wisely, the pair had returned to the intimacy that had served them so well in *Angel in the Wings.* Their antics (all the show actually had going for it) and some forcing kept the show on the boards for seven months.

Michael Todd's Peep Show came in with the hot weather at the end of June, much as many "summer revues" had half a century or more before. It recalled those old shows, too, with its occasional lavishness and its general mediocrity. But in one respect it was remarkably different, for the leading performers were neither old Broadway regulars nor vaudevillians, but strippers and clowns from the sleazy, dying burlesque stages. Their material caused a brouhaha which forced Todd to delete some of the more salacious shenanigans at the same time it earned the show front-page publicity. The result of the headlines coupled with Todd's astute mixture of Ziegfeldian opulence and Minskyesque tawdriness led to a long run.

Another curious mixture was *Pardon Our French*, in which Olsen and Johnson mingled the looniness of the their preceding successes with some bows to a higher theatrical order, including one serious ballet and music by the distinguished Victor Young. The public refused to buy.

Bless You All, the year's final offering, was more traditional. It featured such accomplished comedians as Pearl Bailey, Mary McCarty, and Jules Munshin, along with a dancer of exceptional feline grace, Valerie Bettis. Unfortunately, once again the comedy and music were not up to snuff. The best moment came at the end of the first act when the cast gathered to demonstrate what television could do for political campaigns. Politics were seen to be more than ever merely an adjunct to show business with George Washington and Abraham Lincoln returning to offer commercials plugging their favorite candidates.

Except for two Yiddish revues, *Bagels and Yox* and *Borscht Capades*, which opened a week apart in September, and *Razzle Dazzle*, which had been offered earlier arena-style in a hotel ballroom, 1951 brought in only a single revue. It was another of the many revues of the era which looked better on paper than across the footlights. *Two on the Aisle* had some pleasant Jule Styne songs, such as "Give a Little, Get a Little Love" and "If You Hadn't, But You Did," put across by the tough-fibered Dolores Gray. It also had sketches mostly by Betty Comden and Adolph Green, designed with Bert Lahr, the last great surviving oldtime male clown, in mind, and, indeed, his startled-eyed mugging and caterwauling provided the show with most of its best moments. He cavorted as a boozy baseball veteran saying all the wrong things on a children's radio program, an ex-vaudevillian "reduced" to singing Sieg-fried at the Met, and a mentally myopic streetcleaner wildly filling his bag with $100 bills rather than lose a token award for collecting the most trash. Several critics felt he had not been offered such good revue material since the thirties. But somehow things did not quite add up to the old magic, although, with the forcing becoming all too com-monplace, the show chalked up an eight-month run.

Of the three revues to reach Broadway in 1952 two were hits, and even the flop was uncommonly fascinating. The two hits came first. *New Faces of* 1952 arrived late in the 1951–52 season—almost another summer show. It was instantly recognized as the best in the series to date, and after three more editions appeared in later years, was seen as the unquestioned champion. The new faces included those of Robert Clary, Alice Ghostley, Ronny Graham, Eartha Kitt, Carol Lawrence, and Paul Lynde—most of whom went on to bigger if not better things. Although the production had a certain visual appeal and several pleasant romantic numbers—among them "Love Is a Simple Thing"—it fol-lowed the pattern of most of the better postwar revues, excelling in comedy (including comic songs). In fact, two of the comic songs are classics of the American musical revue: "Monotonous" was the litany of a spoiled, jaded lady who has watched traffic stop for her, caused a panic in the stock market, and had President Truman play bop to please her. The slinky cat-like Miss Kitt on a luxurious couch turned it into a show-stopper. Alice Ghostley did the same for "The Boston Beguine," lamenting that Boston is a city in which the Casbah is merely an Irish bar used for clandestine meetings by the D.A.R. Almost as good was the concerted "Lizzie Borden" in which singers assured audiences "you can't chop your poppa up in Massachusetts." Among the non-musical highlights was the bandaged Paul Lynde's monologue, delivered on crutches, telling of a recent African safari with his "late" wife. So good was the show that even television could not hurt it, so it enjoyed the longest run of any revue in seasons—just under a year.

Yet the virtues and success of this *New Faces* could not obscure the fact that both as art form and as salable entertainment the revue was in deep trouble. The next revue to arrive was the first of several over ensuing seasons that would attempt to find a solution to the problem. In this case the solution, while sometimes hugely successful in the short run, avoided the basic difficulties, for the new entry was *An Evening with Beatrice Lillie*, essentially a one-woman show. The idea of a one-woman or one-man show was nothing really new. Maurice Chevalier, to cite one notable example, had offered them before. Even the non-musical theatre had welcomed such monologuists as Ruth Draper in solo evenings. But the truth was that as far as the musical theatre was concerned, solo shows, albeit they usually had one or two other performers in the cast to assist the star or allow a brief rest or costume change, were essentially nothing but extended vaudeville turns. As such they could respond to a few needs of the modern musical theatre. First of all, with the decline of great skit and songwriters the charismatic star could be expected to triumph over less adept new material when not offering old favorites. Second, these shows would be relatively low budget—easier both to produce and to keep going—in an era when the economic crunch was becoming more painful. Perhaps without realizing it, solo shows also pointed the way to another future answer, at least where long established favorites were involved, for by resorting to bygone hits the shows could serve as retrospectives.

Miss Lillie needed no introduction to playgoers or critics. She was the best and most beloved stage comedienne of the day. Much of her program resurrected old routines and songs, but they were still sharp enough and her skills still so beautifully honed that the numbers seemed singularly fresh—indeed fresher than some of the new items she introduced. Old or new, audiences came prepared. One critic noted, "You know the styles—the rowdy, impudent servant girl, the overbearing lady of fashion, the imposing prima donna with an ornately feathered fan." As such she devastated an actress's first night, using the actress's hair brush to clean her own dirty shoes, and played havoc with a deadpan singer bellowing a love song to her. Assisting her was Reginald Gardiner, up to his old tricks of imitating trains, bringing wallpaper to life, and singing all the parts of a three-part song at the same time.

Much was expected of the year's last revue, *Two's Company*. After all, it had music by Vernon Duke, lyrics by Ogden Nash, and skits by, among others, Peter DeVries. It also had such skillful supporting players as David Burns and Hiram Sherman. However, for many regular play-goers and others who attended the theatre only rarely, its consummate attraction was supposed to be its star, Bette Davis, so long of Hollywood. Alas, the songs were not memorably melodic and the comedy at best fitfully funny, usually only when the supporting comedians were in charge. As a result, *Two's Company* had a rather brief career.

By the next year Bea Lillie's success had prompted a rash of similar shows. Three opened within a month in the fall of 1953. *Anna Russell's Little Show* came first, bringing with it a lady new to Broadway but long popular with those who knew her riotously funny recordings. She made hash of all sorts of popular songs and even harked back to present her one-woman version of an antediluvian type of operetta, "The Prince of Philadelphia." She lasted only a couple of weeks, one week less than *At Home with Ethel Waters.* Accompanied only by a pianist, and dressed in an elegant evening gown, the great black singing-actress spent the evening offering songs she had made famous and other standards.

For a while it seemed as if the next show might run forever. This time the star was a man, the Danish-born pianist and comedian Victor Borge, who called his show *Comedy in Music* and who regaled his patrons with such oddities as Chopin intermingled with "Mary Had a Little Lamb" and with such one-liners as "The Baldwin company has asked me to announce that this is a Steinway piano."

By contrast the year's remaining revue was a patent throwback. Its guiding light was John Murray Anderson, who had played such an important role in the era of the extravagant revue, not only creating the *Greenwich Village Follies* but mounting many other memorable shows. One of his early productions was his 1929 *John Murray Anderson's Almanac* and that, a quarter of a century later, was the name he gave his new offering. Even in 1929 the day of the extravaganza was fading as was the day of the annual, so by 1953 there was no thought of attaching a date to the title and even the opulence had to be cut down—as much or more for economic reasons as for aesthetic ones. Still, always excepting the lack of great, memorable songs that playgoers no longer could count on in revues, this was a mighty good show.

Reduced as the opulence may have been, it was nonetheless lovely to behold. Anderson played brilliantly with lighting effects to create changing harlequinade backdrops, and for his "The Nightingale and the Rose" ballet (revived from a *Greenwich Village Follies*) he bedecked the stage in whites, pearl grays, and silver. Although the musical side was undistinguished it was pleasant enough. Richard Adler and Jerry Ross, who would soon move on to greater scores, composed most of the music, and they had Polly Bergen to put over their songs, while Harry Belafonte, who provided his own songs, came up with at least one passing hit, "Hold 'Em, Joe."

Once again, however, it was comedy which led the way. A London favorite, Hermione Gingold, had superlative material for her American debut and capitalized on every bit of it, abetted handsomely by a fine American film comedian, Billy DeWolfe. She won her audience the moment she came on, telling them how awed she was by New York harbor's fine statue of Judith Anderson. Later she played a frustrated old cellist ("a twang here—a twang there"), grateful for any instrument between her legs, and sang about her perplexity determining "Which Witch" was which. With DeWolfe she portrayed a tippling tourist going to visit an aunt in Ceylon. They also combined their gifts in a sketch that was immediately hailed as a classic. "Dinner for One" found Miss Gingold as a ninety-year-old grande dame seated at the end of a long, elegantly set dining table. Her decrepit butler, played by DeWolfe, had set places for four of her long dead admirers. He moved from chair to chair and in each stead proposed a toast to the lady, then cleared the dishes, reset the table, and started the toasts again. By the third or fourth course he was quite woozy and clattering the dishes. At the end of the multicoursed dinner, he escorted his mistress to her room, though which one was less steady of foot was moot. It may not sound like much, but it was unquestionably one of the most brilliantly performed bits in all of American revue. A young monologuist, Orson Bean, was also on hand at times to offer his own brand of wit.

The show tallied 229 performances, far more than many of the great revues of bygone days attained. But worsening theatrical economics saw the production close still heavily in the red. Nothing quite like it, at least nothing with quite its class, would ever be attempted again. Much of the problem was financial, but changing tastes were equally to blame. Opulence was all but out of style, and within a few years an affected shabbiness would be the mode not merely in the theatre but away from it as well. Nor, for some reason, did the theatre-going public still admire great clowning as much as it once did. Neither Miss Gingold nor DeWolfe would have the sort of stage careers they might have enjoyed had they appeared on the scene twenty or thirty years before.

Of 1954, the less said the better. Only two very short-lived revues raised their curtains. The first was *Hayride*, a "Hillbilly" revue which made the mistake of offering New Yorkers country music and such fine country performers as Lester Flatt and Earl Scruggs a decade or so before they were to become chic in Manhattan. The second was *Blues, Ballads and Sin-Songs*, a one-woman show which brought Libby Holman back to Broadway after a long absence.

No fewer than seven revues opened in 1955. Five can be quickly dismissed. A "diversion in song and dance" called *3 for Tonight* had only five performers, but since four of them were Harry Belafonte, Marge and Gower Champion, and Hiram Sherman, the show actually recorded a profit in its two-month run. *Almost Crazy* and *Catch a Star!* were traditional if singularly inept revues. Solo productions offered Maurice Chevalier and the droll English comedienne Joyce Grenfell. The two noteworthy revues were unusual in that neither was exactly a mainstream Broadway mounting. February saw the *Shoestring Revue* premiere at a tiny off-Broadway type house in the heart of the theatre district, while *Phoenix '55* opened at what had once been the Yiddish Art Theatre, a fine standard-size house far down on Second Avenue. Typically for revues of their period they produced no enduring songs, but excelled at comedy. Indeed the *Shoestring Revue* (and its successor, *Shoestring '57*) was among the most unfailingly witty and hilarious assemblages ever conceived. A man alone in a hotel room and "In Bed with the Reader's Digest" peruses articles with such titles as "The Eleventh Baby Is the Easiest" and "We're Bringing Up Our Children Like Poodles," and finally is persuaded to jump from the room's window when another article promises him sex in afterlife. The Greek tragedy

Medea was reduced to a Walt Disney cartoon. Group psychoanalysis was shown to need all the therapy it could get. The revue was the creation of a young man from Vermont, Ben Bagley, who went on to produce several other notable revues, all more or less off-Broadway, and later to produce a series of notable recordings of forgotten Broadway music. Among the many great talents given a leg up by this show were Beatrice Arthur, Dody Goodman, Arte Johnson, Chita Rivera, and, best of all, a brilliant little lady harlequin who died all too young, Dorothy Greener.

An even greater comedienne provided the laughs in *Phoenix '55*, Beatrice Lillie's only true rival, Nancy Walker. She was in top form, whether trapped helplessly in a bucket seat, as a ballerina in a Freudian ballet, or mocking the excesses of the undisciplined method school of acting by impulsively wreaking havoc on scenery and fellow actors.

Bagley was responsible for two of 1956's better revues. The first, which played the same Phoenix at which Nancy Walker had cavorted a year earlier, was *The Littlest Revue*. Contributors included Lee Adams, Vernon Duke, John Latouche, Ogden Nash, Charles Strouse, and Eudora Welty. Its bright, young and talented cast included Joel Grey, Tammy Grimes, and Charlotte Rae. They combined their skills to spoof the inhabitants of an old hotel, want ads, diets, and Olde English ditties. Several critics felt the show was superior in every way to the *Shoestring Revue*. While business was not sufficient to warrant an extension of the originally announced limited run, the show has since developed its own special coterie of admirers.

Although Maggie Smith was one of the *New Faces of 1956* who went on to achieve major celebrity, the show stealer of the production was T. C. Jones, the finest female impersonator since Julian Eltinge. His art was so deft that many in the audience gasped in surprise during the curtain calls when he removed his wig and revealed a bald head. His best moments included a send-up of Tallulah Bankhead and a spoof of the lavish old *Follies*-style numbers. Tiger Haynes, John Reardon, and Inga Swenson were among the other notable newcomers. Unfortunately, the show as a whole marked a perceptible decline from the excellences of the 1952 edition. It ran six months, but closed still in the red.

The year's three other revues were bunched together in November. Ignoring the calendar, the first was Bagley's *Shoestring '57*, a worthy successor to the earlier show, with several of the same performers and all of the same comic brightness. It was followed by *That Girl at the Bijou*, a one-woman show featuring the satiric dancer, Iva Kitchell. From London came *Cranks*, a revue conceived by the noted choreographer John Cranko and with music by John Addison. The cast of four included the then unknown Anthony Newley. However, even this imposing if limited roster could not come up with a satisfactory evening, at least as far as most critics and the general public were concerned.

The two revues that arrived in 1957 were both theatrical bombs. A *Ziegfeld Follies* was mounted in honor of the 50th anniversary of the first edition, but the consensus was the production was not an honor but an insult. The settings and costumes were shabby and unimaginative; there were only, depending on the night, six or eight chorus girls (Ziegfeld regularly had sixty or more in his heyday), and the material was dreadful. Lost in the mishmash were such fine performers as Billy DeWolfe, Harold Lang, Carol Lawrence, and, horror of horrors, Beatrice Lillie. No better was a one-man (or was it one-woman?) revue, *Mask and Wig*, with the wig again hiding T. C. Jones's bald head. Regrettably, his material was not all that good. Moreover, if the great clowns could no longer assure a musical's run it was highly unlikely that a female impersonator could. Critics and playgoers, however much they might admit enjoying lighthearted performers, were insisting on substance more than talent, text more than personality. Jones's early death left unanswered what sort of future the theatre could have offered him. That answer probably would not have been kind.

The Next President, 1958's first revue, featured the political barbs of Mort Sahl, a dancer named Anneliese Widman, and some folk singers. Calling itself a "Musical Salmagundi," it pretentiously labeled each act; Act One being called "The Status Quo"; Act Two, "A Brand New Attitude with the Same Old Prejudices." The nonsense ran less than two weeks.

A brilliant French revue, which had also delighted London, came in during the fall. Playgoers needed no French to enjoy *La Plume de Ma Tante*, for most of the riotous skits were wordless and what little explanation was required was offered wrily by the show's creator and compère, Robert Dhery. Both the show and Dhery recalled a Russian success of the 1920s, *Chauve-Souris*, with its droll compère, Nikita Balieff. The new show's highlight was its first-act finale, in which a group of monks enter quietly singing "Frère Jacques" and begin pulling bell ropes. Bit by bit the music grows faster until the curtain falls on the wildly swinging monks.

It would be wrong to call the year's final offering a one-man or one-woman show or even a solo show, since a pair of brilliant comics held the stage all night long. But this pair was multi-talented, becoming eventually Broadway's most durable lyricists and librettists. So not surprisingly, *A Party with Betty Comden and Adolph Green* relied heavily on material from their earlier shows. Its low budget allowed it to make a profit despite a short run.

A pleasant but unexceptional mounting, *The Billy Barnes Revue*, and a solo show starring Frenchman Yves Montand began 1959's brief parade. More interesting was *At the Drop of a Hat*, a two-man show from London, in which hefty, bearded Michael Flanders delivered his civilized humor from the confines of his wheelchair and joined the clean-cut, professorial Donald Swann, who played piano, in Edward Learish songs. In a small way the show moved a step toward a new kind of revue, for though songs constituted a good part of the evening none was a typical revue number. There were no love songs, no songs suggesting lavish productions. They were merely lyrics to which melodies had been added as a sort of sugar coating. In an uncompromising theatre the pair might well have offered simply an evening of lyric readings, but poetry or lyric readings do not chalk up long runs, so Broadway compromised. Yet the texts, those lyrics and the interlarded comments, were the heart of the evening. Thus, Flanders and Swann were acknowledging what had long been obvious. Superior melodies were a thing of the past in American musical revue. Several shows in future seasons would carry this departure even further, virtually to the seemingly logical conclusion of a revue without music. But, even more so than the solo show, this could not be a definitive answer to the genre's woes. It was utterly lacking the requisite balance.

One more attempt to resuscitate the traditional revue was seen in *The Girls Against the Boys*, which starred "two royal mountebanks of show business," Bert Lahr and Nancy Walker. For the umpteenth time, however, the stars were better than their material. They shone as a pair of rock and rollers and as a hostile but totally silent husband and wife. Miss Walker also played a groveling Japanese war bride who learns American wives do not grovel; while Lahr was an uproariously pathetic stagedoor Johnny who finds the only bit of femininity in the chorus is a swishy chorus boy. Mounted with no particular panache and filled with lackluster songs, the show folded quickly. Playgoers again reasserted their refusal to make allowances for an unbalanced entertainment, great clowns or no.

To the economically pressed Broadway of its day, the closing of *The Girls Against the Boys* passed as merely another costly mistake. In retrospect it can be seen as something more—an obscure, sad milestone as the revue apparently approached the end of its road. The show was the last revue for both its stars, and although a fine comedienne such as Hermione Gingold would appear in a 1960 failure she was a newcomer to America and the remainder of her career here was rocky. So *The Girls Against the Boys* marked the final occasion when names of great "oldtimers" (even if Miss Walker was then only in her late thirties) were displayed above the title of an "old time" revue. Things were changing or deteriorating. You could take your choice.

There were few revues in the 1960s and even fewer in the 1970s. Few revues in the 1960s ran long, fewer still were commercial successes. What's more, all of the longer runs and more profitable entertainments displayed the new look that several recent productions had pioneered. They were usually slimmed-down affairs, often featuring scanty casts (with no choruses), even more scanty scenery, and a new approach to the balance of substance. There was, for example, precious little new music in the best of these shows and what there was left behind absolutely nothing memorable. To a large extent these revues succeeded or failed not on their splendor or their melodies, but on their wit. The carefully contrived balance of the great old revues was nowhere in evidence.

In a book called *American Musical Revue* the decade's very first revue sneaks in here almost by courtesy, since it had no songs at all, albeit four jazz musicians on one side of the stage sometimes punctuated the humor with a few bars of melody and played as the panels that served as scenery were shifted about. True, the music was by the noted jazz artist Don Elliott, and the opening number was called "Word Dance," but A *Thurber Carnival* was essentially what Louis Kronenberger pithily called "a one-mind show" and that mind belonged to the odd-ball, widely popular James Thurber. With a brilliant cast that included Tom Ewell, Alice Ghostley, Paul Ford, and Peggy Cass, Thurber's humor was hilariously personified. The cast brought to life every manner of matter from the small, foolish daydreams of Walter Mitty to the surviving flower that prompts civilization to rise from its ashes and build anew, until civilization destroys itself again, and again leaves only one last flower. However, Thurber's humor, unlike ferris wheels and cotton candy, could not be readily duplicated, so when the show closed its seven-month-run (interrupted by a long summer vacation) and packed its bags to move on, no similar carnival could take over the grounds. Theatrically, this one-mind show was a one-shot phenomenon.

The year also brought in two small-scale but traditional revues, both of which were short-lived. *From A to Z* featured Miss Gingold and offered the work of such rising young talents as Woody Allen and Jerry Herman, none of whom would ever again do major work in revues on Broadway. *Vintage '60* was a California show imported with disastrous results by the usually knowing David Merrick. Mention of Herman, however, brings up an interesting point, for New Yorkers first became acquainted with his writing in off-Broadway revues. Throughout these years off-Broadway continued to present tiny revues of varying merit. One or two will be mentioned later in passing, but for the most part these shows never left the confines of off-Broadway or had any significant influence on mainstream theatre, the way some earlier ones had. Possibly they deserve examination somewhere. Not here.

As it had been in A *Thurber Carnival*, music was relegated to the background in another superb, more intimate entertainment, *An Eve-*

ning with Mike Nichols and Elaine May. In sometimes improvised "duologues" the pair kidded everything from telephone service to Tennessee Williams plays (whose heroines were given to "drink, prostitution, and puttin' on airs").

The only other 1960 revue was also a failure. *Laughs and Other Events* was a one-man show displaying the warm, diverse talents of Stanley Holloway, a fine English comedian who had endeared himself to Broadway in *My Fair Lady*. He included numbers from his music hall days, but neither his material nor his art was sufficient to sustain an entire evening on its own.

A one-woman show, *Show Girl*, ushered in 1961. The woman was Carol Channing, and much of her material was not new either. In one of her best moments she compared the old-style musical comedy with the modern musical play. To represent the older shows she culled songs from *Lend an Ear's* spoof of 1920s' musicals, "The Gladiola Girl," juxtaposing them with imaginary examples from Rodgers and Hammerstein-like endeavors. Thus, "Join Us in a Little Cup of Tea" was paired with "This Is a Darned Fine Funeral." Low-budget to begin with and carefully husbanded financially, the show's three-month New York stand and a successful tour allowed it to close in the black.

Later in the year Billy Barnes returned with *The Billy Barnes People*, all of whom waved goodbye after less than a week. Far more interesting was an arrival from Chicago's answer to off-Broadway, *From the Second City*. Once again music (and scenery) took a distinctly back seat. In the hands of such superior young comics as Barbara Harris and Alan Arkin, laughter was the order of the night. Skits made mincemeat of such seemingly touchy topics as vestiges of Nazism in Germany and the possible horrors of the first 100 days of a Goldwater administration.

In 1962 a new edition of *New Faces* came quickly a cropper, while Eddie Fisher and Jack Benny appeared at the Winter Garden and Ziegfeld respectively in entertainments that blurred the line between one-man shows and vaudeville. The year's best revue showed that when wit was the heart of the evening the English were capable of making us seem amateurs. *Beyond the Fringe* might be considered an English first cousin of *From the Second City*. It featured four young British university graduates—Alan Bennett, Jonathan Miller, Dudley Moore, and Peter Cook. They were unknown to Americans when the show opened, but all four, especially the first three, moved on to fame and fortune. Their skits, dialogues, and monologues took devastating aim at such light-hearted matters as atomic holocausts, racism, and politics. Bennett made comic hash of a Sunday sermon, Miller discoursed maliciously on pornography, Cook portrayed a dimwitted miner who had wanted to be a judge, and all four young men combined to make more hash of Shakespearean clichés compounded by the absurd stylistic clichés of emotive Shakespearean actors. One of the few musical moments had Moore, as a concert pianist, trying frantically to finish a piece with every manner of coda.

Possibly because A *Thurber Carnival* had been so rapturously received, 1963's first revue, *The Beast in Me*, went to the author's *Fables of Our Times* to create an evening of songs and skits in which all the performers portrayed animals. Another attempt to broaden the nature of revue, it lasted half a week. *The Golden Age*, "An entertainment in the words and music of the Elizabethan Age," did almost twice that.

Josephine Baker, the black American singer who had been the darling of Paris between the wars, returned briefly in 1964 in a one-woman show. Much of her early fire had gone, but nostalgia and sentiment granted her a small audience. From Paris, too, came a somewhat tacky version of the *Folies Bergere*, which survived on the strength of its name for nearly six months. The British fared a little better, at least artistically, with *Oh, What a Lovely War!* which offered a potpourri of World War I songs, music-hall tricks, and a thin story line to indict the callousness and fatuousness of bygone warriors and politicians. It ran less than four months. An uneven, six-character London revue, *Cambridge Circus*, might have had an even shorter run had it not taken the unusual step of transferring from Broadway to off-Broadway. Last, but certainly not least in 1964, was the return of Victor Borge in *Comedy in Music Opus 2*, the year's most economical, longest run (six months) revue.

Only one revue reached Broadway in 1965, apart from the return of Maurice Chevalier in a one-man show and one curiosity. The new revue, like Chevalier, had a Gallic flavor. *La Grosse Valise*, by Robert

Dhery of *La Plume de ma Tante* fame, was perceived as an unworthy sequel to the earlier hit and survived a mere week. The curiosity was *This Was Burlesque*, which had been playing for several years off-Broadway. With Ann Corio as star, this slightly dowdy re-creation of a dowdy genre in its heyday added four more months on Broadway to its record. But off-Broadway was looking back not only at the raffish if often dubious delights of burlesque. It was also looking back at the work of one of our musical masters. In one respect *The Decline and Fall of the Entire World as Seen Through the Eyes of Cole Porter Revisited* may be viewed as an attempt to answer the problem of what to do with the revue when the number of outstanding composers appeared to be dwindling and the surviving greats were devoting themselves to book shows. In effect, the answer provided by the often imaginative maverick, Ben Bagley, was to resurrect the best of their portfolios in a superior retrospective. The result was further fragmenting of the now almost moribund revue genre. Side by side with one-man shows and revues which lived by their wits we would now have a form that could be called such names as "portfolio revues," "retrospectives," or "celebrations." The new show sang Porter songs from his earliest Broadway efforts to 1950 and sang them in roughly chronological order, with some bits of spoken "continuity" in between. Bagley set aside most well-known standards, leaving it instead to Kaye Ballard to stop the show with a saga, "The Tale of the Oyster," recounting the unusual results of some unusual social ambition, and Carmen Alvarez to kick up a storm of applause by kicking off her shoes to sing "Find Me a Primitive Man." Given the great material that Porter and many of his contemporaries had left behind it was clear that, skillfully handled, such entertainments could provide delightful evenings. At the same time, much like many of the one-man shows, these offerings, however wonderful, had to have a trace of museum mustiness about them, as well as more than a tinge of desperation. They also confessed to a certain lack of feeling for theatrical history on Broadway and Broadway's failure to offer regular revivals from our older stages. Apart from *Show Boat, Porgy and Bess*, and *Pal Joey* nothing from the musical catalogue before *Oklahoma!* is revived with any regularity, and the older shows which are brought back on occasion are generally offered in bloated, savagely rewritten versions. Opera houses around the world, and especially in America, may be living museums for an art form that is basically dead, but at least they attempt the whole range of operatic history. Broadway has nothing comparable. The better old musical comedies, for all their gorgeous, hit-filled scores, are dismissed for their naive books. The idea of reviving a great old revue is waved away even more vehemently on the grounds that skits were too frequently topical. One wonders, though, if topicality is truly that ephemeral. How much of *The Band Wagon* or *As Thousands Cheer* is really that dated? Take the latter. Assuredly the more knowing people who often constitute the remaining audience for live theatre, can recall the satirized foibles of Herbert Hoover, Gandhi, John D. Rockefeller, Aimee Semple McPherson, or Noel Coward. Even as this is being written a young Southerner has been sentenced to death for lynching a black. So is "Supper Time" no longer meaningful or poignant? Have the sacheted charms of a hundred-year-old Fifth Avenue Easter parade receded beyond recall? Whatever the response, the modern retrospective revue, like so many other attempts to find new byways for the genre, can only lead to a dead end. For all the great composers who graced Broadway, their number was definitely finite and so are the possibilities of culling from their achievements. Yet *The Decline and Fall*, etc. ran nine months, has enjoyed revivals around the country, and was made into a popular recording. And it was eventually followed by other successful portfolio revues.

In 1965, *Wait a Minim'*, a revue that had been successful in its South African homeland and in London, enjoyed a long run. Its cast of eight whites kidded their country's racial policy but spent most of the evening offering folk songs and anecdotes. As if by contrast the American *A Hand Is on the Gate* presented black poetry and folk song, and had only a brief run. Gilbert Becaud came from France for a one-man show, while *Let's Sing Yiddish* followed the vogue for assemblages of folk material, this time taken from Jewish sources. The year closed with the return of Flanders and Swann in the appropriately entitled *At the Drop of Another Hat*, which did not quite recapture the charm or success of their first show but nonetheless was a hit.

Except for two more Jewish offerings, *Hello, Solly!* (its title obviously capitalizing on the success of *Hello, Dolly!*) and *Sing, Israel, Sing*, not a single revue raised its curtain on Broadway in 1967. However, Judy Garland, Eddie Fisher, Buddy Hackett, and Marlene Dietrich all appeared in vaudevilles. That off-Broadway was still active and still no longer influencing Broadway could be seen in the success at the tiny Cherry Lane of *In Circles*. The composer was Al Carmines, who for some seasons received widespread press coverage, but never found a niche in the big time.

In January of 1968 *Jacques Brel Is Alive and Well and Living in Paris* began a run of 1,800 performances downtown. The show made an evening of the songs of the popular Belgian composer. A cast of four featured a memorable performance by Elly Stone. It was the second successful retrospective, thus reinforcing the burgeoning vogue for such shows. And to the extent that both this and the Porter show were off-Broadway enterprises, it belies the generalization that off-Broadway could not lead the way in musical theatre. The show was called a "cabaret revue" and was presented at the popular Village Gate. As such it recalled to a small extent the cabaret revues that had flourished before Prohibition on the rooftops of such theatres as the Casino, the New Amsterdam, and the Century. But those revues had mirrored in miniature the larger offerings downstairs, while the modern cabaret shows in Greenwich Village and elsewhere were scarcely less intimate and simple than the frugal modern Broadway presentations.

Broadway itself offered nothing to boast about during the year. There was another Israeli presentation, *The Grand Music Hall of Israel*, a final and failed edition of *New Faces*, and the first mainstream retrospective, the unsuccessful *Noel Coward's Sweet Potato*. And, of course, there were a number of short-lived one-man or one-woman shows.

Matters were even worse in 1969 when only two revues appeared. *Trumpets of the Lord*, a collection of black hymns and sermons, had done well off-Broadway and on tour, but Broadway would have none of it. *The New Music Hall of Israel* managed a two-month stand. However, off-Broadway came up with a notorious revue that has become one of the phenomena of our theatrical history, *Oh! Calcutta!* For several seasons nudity had been developing into a stage fad. Especially off-Broadway, but on Broadway too, every possible pretext (and sometimes no pretext at all) had been used to bring on undressed men and women. This was not the carefully posed, suggestive nudity of the Ziegfeld era or the somewhat more mobile, now seemingly tame, nudity which often got Earl Carroll and others into trouble. This was blatant, frequently frontal nudity, wriggling and writhing for its own sake. All sense of order, decorum, and decency had seemingly fled the theatre. And no show trafficked in nudity so blatantly or so writhingly as *Oh! Calcutta!* To add insult to injury, it was even announced that the title was derived from a dirty phrase, and that the phrase was French mattered little. Surprisingly, the revue was the brainchild of an often distinguished English drama critic, Kenneth Tynan. And his list of contributors included such hallowed names as Samuel Beckett and Jules Feiffer. More surprising still were the number of responsible critics who, while condeming the material as sophomoric, insisted that the nudity was the least offensive part of the show and, to some, a legitimate attraction. In itself, of course, there is absolutely nothing wrong with nudity, even on stage occasionally. But in the feverish excitement of the day there was something obscene about the way shows flaunted and promoted their nude scenes. And *Oh! Calcutta!* was happier than most to make noise about its skin show. Even the staidly liberal *Times* succumbed, although its ready-to-be-pleased critic, Clive Barnes, clearly had mixed feelings. While he noted that "This is the kind of show to give pornography a dirty name," he was really complaining about the "failure of the writers and the producers." The nude scenes, he insisted, "while derivative, were attractive enough." Another critic claimed, "Innocence, sheer *innocence* is the quality produced on stage by total nudity, no matter how suggestive the material being offered," only to add, "in the salacious *Oh! Calcutta!* innocent nakedness is entirely *in*appropriate and tended to defeat the show's purpose." Despite criticism, and no doubt because of the highly hyped salaciousness, the original *Oh! Calcutta!* went on to compile a stand of 1,314 performances, including a move to Broadway in 1971. In 1976 the revue was revived in a small theatre at a Broadway hotel and, at this writing, still apparently playing to profitable houses, has far surpassed the run of the earlier production. From the Jews and the blacks, two always spunky forces in American theatre, came 1970's pair of revues. *Light, Lively and Yiddish* was a trite affair, done in Yiddish with an English-speaking compère. It had a modest run. Far more beguiling and successful was *The Me Nobody Knows*. Actually, the finished, polished show was the work of white authors, but they took their basic material from the writings of New York's underprivileged school children, mostly black or Hispanic. These compositions were set to folk-rock music. Songs told of harrowing brushes with the law and with drugs, of innocent but hurtful bigotry, and of the often seemingly transient happier moments of ghetto living. A touching, unusual evening in the theatre, it began life off-Broadway, but its good press and word-of-mouth quickly brought it uptown, where it continued a run that eventually lasted a year and a half.

The same two ethnic groups were the source of 1971's revues. Melvin Van Peebles's *Ain't Supposed To Die a Natural Death*, although said to have a "book," was essentially a series of vignettes offering various black perspectives on life. Peebles made some attempt to balance his picture. Unfortunately, the scales were tilted too much toward venting black hatreds. As a result it was hardly a pleasant show, a far cry from the innocuous bygone revues. Nonetheless it found a substantial audience. So did both Israeli revues, *To Live Another Summer, To Pass Another Winter* and *Only Fools Are Sad*.

A pair of American revues arrived early in 1972. *That's Entertainment*, a botched retrospective of Howard Dietz and Arthur Schwartz songs, lasted only four performances, but one more evening of black viewpoints, *Don't Bother Me, I Can't Cope*, was popular both in New York and on tour. One reason for its success was that its author, Micki Grant, was able to mute the often repellent hostility heard in Peebles's work. She was not quite as original as Peebles, sometimes setting her lyrics to well-known melodies, but her sunnier disposition prevailed. Later in the year a pair of foreign revues, *From Israel with Love* and *Pacific Paradise*, the latter a Maori mounting from New Zealand, quickly came and left, as did a curious bit of ecological preaching, *Mother Earth*.

Off-Broadway was still having better luck with retrospectives in 1973 than Broadway. Uptown *Nash at Nine*, setting Ogden Nash's verse to music, had a brief run, while downtown *Oh, Coward!* and *Berlin to Broadway with Kurt Weill* enjoyed longer stands. At the end of the year on Broadway *Good Evening*, a two-man show featuring Peter Cook and Dudley Moore of *Beyond the Fringe*, began a season-long run. Highlights included a skit about a restaurant serving only two specialties— frogs and peaches—and Moore as a one-legged Tarzan. *An Evening with Josephine Baker* could muster only a week's business.

Not much can be said of 1974's trio of Broadway entries. Alan Jay Lerner offered his "cavalcade of American music," *Music! Music!*, but Broadway wouldn't buy it any more than it would Sammy Cahn's retrospective of his own material, *Words and Music*. Sammy was essentially another one-man show, headlining Sammy Davis, Jr.

Nor was 1975 productive. A popular singer, Harry Chapin, starred in his own *The Night That Made America Famous*, which featured mostly protest songs, while the kooky Bette Midler, assisted by Lionel Hampton, was largely responsible for the eleven-week stay of *Clams on the Half Shell*, presented as a cabaret at the huge Minskoff Theatre and heavily amplified. Even all the glorious songs in another portfolio revue, *Rodgers and Hart*, could not earn it an extended run. *Me and Bessie* offered Linda Hopkins singing songs identified with Bessie Smith. The last revue of the year, *A Musical Jubilee*, purported to offer a history of songs from American musical theatre, but many of the songs on the program, such as "Mademoiselle from Armentiers," had scant, if any, real connection with our lyric stage. Probably only a remarkable cast which included Lillian Gish, Tammy Grimes, Larry Kert, Patrice Munsel, John Raitt, Cyril Ritchard, and Dick Shawn can account for its three-month run.

Despite an occasional commercial success and some interesting, if frequently abrasive material, the health of the American musical revue in these years was disheartening. The very nature of the shows—solo shows, ethnic shows, retrospective potpourris, shows relying on sensational nudity—suggested that there continued to be myriad problems. Perhaps the most immediate was simply a loss of interest in the tradsitional revue genre. Reasons for this were catalogued earlier, but they can hardly be a final answer. After all, in an ailing Broadway, a Broadway in which even several long-standing composers can no longer find an outlet, surely someone somewhere could have decided to have a fling with a good, old-fashioned revue. Perhaps, although it would be hard for them or anyone else to admit, the great veterans were written out. It is generally conceded that we lack today the veritable army of masterful composers with which we were blessed between the world wars and for a time thereafter. And are there no young, clever skit-writers to turn to? Many of the off-Broadway revues of the last several decades tell us there are any number of superior writers awaiting a chance on Broadway. New Broadway revues could be as witty if not as memorably melodic as they once were. Of course rarely does beauty come cheap, and the horrendous economic crunch would no doubt restrain the opulence that for so long had enriched the revue. But millions have been found for lavish book musicals, so why not millions for an occasional revue? Gone, of course, are virtually all of the great old clowns, and neither performers nor training grounds for new clowns have emerged to fill their shoes. Moreover, is there still an audience for the traditional revue? The last decade has not answered that question unequivocally but has more than hinted that the answer is "yes." And where there are playgoers to plunk down their dollars at the box office there should always be a theatre ready to offer the entertainment they want. Let's look at that last decade and see what it might mean to the future of the American revue.

10

What's Past Is Epilogue

Years from now, when we look back on our theatrical history, we may recognize the arrival and success of *Bubbling Brown Sugar* in 1976 as a turning point in the saga of the American musical revue. It will be a strange, not especially prominent landmark, for *Bubbling Brown Sugar* in so many respects was an unexceptional show. Certainly it was not the trailblazer that the 1894 *Passing Show* was. Nor was it the stunning exemplar that Ziegfeld made of his greatest *Follies*. It lacked the commanding originality and shimmering brilliance of *Charlot's Revue,* which led to the more streamlined and thoughtful revues of the 1930s. And it had none of the great stars, unforgettable new melodies, careful opulence, or sustained wit that the great American revues of the 1930s offered. Indeed, there were none of the uproarious skits that punctuated the best of the old revues. Instead, in a throwback that went far back, there was a "book" with a very loose story line to tie the songs together. Many of the songs were new, but the ones that set feet tapping and sent audiences out humming were old, for at heart *Bubbling Brown Sugar* was the first hugely successful retrospective revue mounted on Broadway. However, it was not a retrospective celebrating the work of a single. composer. Rather, it was a paean to an era and a place—to the long-gone Harlem of between the world wars. This was the Harlem to which hedonistic, carefree, or uncaring whites bedecked in tuxedos, evening gowns, furs, and jewels went slumming, and in which blacks, deprived and shunned elsewhere, put on a happy face and made the world a better place for a few hours each evening. It was the Harlem that delighted in the songs of Bert Williams, Shelton Brooks, Eubie Blake, "Fats" Waller, and Duke Ellington, all of whom were represented on the program and several of whom would be heard from again, importantly and soon.

Delighted critics unwittingly resorted to the very phrases once lavished on the black revues of the 1920s, when the phrases, however well-intentioned, implicitly evoked racial stereotypes. Basically they were directed at what whites saw as the blacks' singular gift for exuberant rhythms, for their glittering, compelling façade of razzmatazz, and for their uplifting energy (at least when they were dancing). Black revues of the twenties were almost always perceived as "dancing shows." Because audiences were as delighted as the critics, *Bubbling Brown Sugar* ran just short of two years and was popular on the road and abroad.

Apart from one-woman shows featuring Shirley MacLaine and Debbie Reynolds, the year's only other revue, *Your Arm's Too Short To Box with God*, was also black, at once totally different and very similar. Like its predecessor, it had a "story line"—this time taken from the Gospel According to St. Matthew, and, like its predecessor, its revivalistic fervor was greeted with huzzahs, such as the one that noted it "rollicks with contagious high spirits." But religion, not secular escape, was the basis for its high spirits, and since for playgoers religion rarely has the appeal that more mundane frippery has, the show ran only half as long as *Bubbling Brown Sugar*. But still a year's run on Broadway was no mean achievement.

Ipi-Tombi, the first revue of 1977, was also black, and had been a smash hit in London. However, since it was an assemblage of dances from South Africa it quickly became embroiled in politics. Picketed by some liberals and given a cold shoulder by most critics, it failed to duplicate its West End success. Oddly enough, in a footnote to black theatrical history, the show was the last to play the Harkness Theatre way up on Broadway above Columbus Circle. In the 1920s, when the house was known as the Colonial, it had been home to many black musicals.

Betty Comden and Adolph Green once again extended invitations to A *Party*, albeit this time the public failed to respond with its earlier enthusiasm. But playgoers did respond to the year's most intellectual revue, a brilliantly executed, low-budget retrospective, *Side by Side by Sondheim*. Although Sondheim is a major figure in American musical theatre, this show, too, had come from London. It was not a show to set feet tapping or to send audiences away whistling, for Sondheim is not that kind of composer. But he is absolutely unique and unmatched as a lyricist (only Alan Jay Lerner at his best is comparable, and his style is markedly different). The result was an entertainment that demanded an audience's riveted attention, a heady evening of unalloyed literacy, wit and, perhaps alloyed, misanthropy.

By contrast *Beatlemania* offered Beatles' fans an evening of heavily amplified rock. The Beatles themselves were not in it, just youngsters imitating them. But that hardly dissuaded aficionados who came in such droves that the show compiled a run of 920 performances. Little mention was made in the press of the fact that the Beatles, more than any other group, had propelled the rock craze in America and that this craze had been the major factor in driving older styles of Broadway music off the airways and eventually denying many of even the best older composers a Broadway market. Toward the end of the year Victor Borge again returned successfully with his one-man show, although probably few young Beatles fans were in his audience.

The failed revues of 1978 were a mixed, if sometimes interesting, bag. A mess called *Elvis the Legend Lives*, centering on the rock idol, Elvis Presley, died quickly and mercifully. Three others had varying merits, although some playgoers might have hesitated to call one or more a revue. A *History of the American Film*, which mixed songs with parodies of famous films, had won high praise on the road. As sometimes happens, however, New Yorkers refused to join in the fun. *Working* set many of Studs Terkel's slices of lower-class life to music.

Elizabeth Swados's *Runaways* employed several actual runaways to sing her songs and recite her speeches about the problems of leaving home. The show had begun off-Broadway and some critics felt it lost part of its flavor and force in the move uptown. Nonetheless, it ran about eight months.

All the other revue hits of 1978 were retrospectives. There were four of them, and they fell into interesting pairs. To call *Dancin'* a retrospective is admittedly stretching a point. But Bob Fosse's superb kaleidoscope of choreography had frequent recourse to the melodies of old favorites, from Bach, John Philip Sousa, and George M. Cohan to more modern composers. The musical became one of the longest-running shows in Broadway history. This could be attributed in no small measure to its excellence as theatre, which lured countless American playgoers. But trade sheets were later to point out another peculiar reason, its appeal to visiting foreigners who spoke no English but wanted to see a Broadway production. As a show which danced from first curtain to last this was just what the visitors were looking for. Its "mate" was *The American Dance Machine*, which re-created famous dance numbers from bygone hits. It was not mounted at a major Broadway house and lacked the scintillating elan of *Dancin'*, but nevertheless chalked up a six-month stand.

The other pair was *Ain't Misbehavin'* and *Eubie!*. *Ain't Misbehavin'* was a salute to the beloved composer and pianist, Thomas "Fats" Waller, and was filled not only with all of his best known compositions but with songs by other composers which he helped popularize. Another small-cost affair, it had first been mounted at the Manhattan Theatre Club and later moved to Broadway. *Eubie!*, of course, celebrated the work of the equally beloved composer, ragtime pianist, and, in the decade or so before his death, irresistible public raconteur, Eubie Blake. Blake himself was only a few years from his 100th birthday when the show was produced. It was a bigger production than *Ain't Misbehavin'*, with a much larger cast and more elaborate production numbers. That it stayed before the footlights less than a third as long as *Ain't Misbehavin'* may have been attributable in part to its higher running costs. It ran just over a year, while the Waller show ran for more than three years.

Together these four shows, certainly the three mainstream shows, consolidated the nature and possibly the drift of the contemporary American musical revue. Perhaps the most notable aspect of these revues was their essential fragmentation. No longer was a revue a balanced mesh of funny sketches, melodic new songs, eye-filling scenery, lively dancing, and—often but not always—great stars. In two of these new shows little but the dancing mattered, in the other two little but the wonderful old songs. None had much sustained, developed laughter. Scenery was minimal in all, and the casts featured primarily young unknowns who had little chance to display any versatility. If the shows had anything in common it was first of all their appeal simply to the good, old-fashioned values of primary entertainment. They were not out to prosyletize or rationalize or explain, but merely to give their audiences a few hours of delightful escape. Second, in varying degrees, they reminded their audiences of the delightful escapism of yesteryear's revues by trafficking in nostalgia. *The American Dance Machine*, *Ain't Misbehavin'*, and *Eubie!*, like *Bubbling Brown Sugar* before them, did this openly and unabashedly; *Dancin'*, with its return to older composers and its modern version of the old "dancing show," more subtly.

In 1979 a two-artist, non-musical revue, *Monteith and Rand*, with John Monteith and Suzanne Rand, delighted playgoers for ten weeks, while *Peter Allen Up in One* provided a less satisfying and less durable solo show. Phyllis Newman ran eleven weeks in her one-woman show, *The Madwoman of Central Park West*, which allowed her to sing some original songs by Kander and Ebb, Leonard Bernstein, Betty Comden and Adolph Green, and others. *Live from New York* was a showcase for television's zany Gilda Radner. One strange offering was *Coquelico*, a "multi-media entertainment" from the National Theatre of Prague. Nor should the Radio City Music Hall be overlooked. The magnificent art deco theatre, once New York's premiere film house, had fallen on hard times and turned to lavish, brainless revues not unlike those once presented down Sixth Avenue at the old Hippodrome.

However, the year's biggest revue hit was another trip down memory lane, although not strictly speaking a retrospective. *Sugar Babies* was a look at the best of old Minsky-style burlesque, albeit with a noted emphasis not on its strippers but its wonderful raunchy comedy. Certainly no Minsky show was ever as expensively, slickly, or stylishly mounted. One had to look to Mike Todd's all-but-forgotten *Star and Garter* for anything approaching it in class. Significantly Todd's production had co-starred the most famous (and cerebral) of all strippers, Gypsy Rose Lee, and the great Broadway roustabout clown, Bobby Clark. The new show also had two stars, Mickey Rooney and Ann Miller, both of whom had gained their fame almost exclusively in films. When a road company was sent out headed by two Broadway favorites, Carol Channing and Robert Morse, the show bombed. Clearly in this instance the old material, not really old Broadway material, was less a lure than the film celebrities. The show was developed by Ralph G. Allen, a college professor with an unashamed love of old bump and grind. But the failure of the road company makes it moot whether he or anyone else could strike gold again, unless some exceptionally potent drawing cards head the bill. Despite the nature of the material, the evening's blend of skits, singing, and dances re-created the feeling of the old revues as much as it did of old burlesque shows, and may have played some small part in its success.

No fewer than eight shows that could be classified as revues appeared in 1980. Most can be quickly discaded. *Your Arm's Too Short . . . ,* was profitably revived. One-man shows and vaudevilles included those headed by Blackstone the Magician, Shelley Berman, and Stephen Wade, whose *Banjo Dancing* was designed to demonstrate his ability with the instrument. *Black Broadway*, whose cast included such popular young and old entertainers as John W. Bubbles, Adelaide Hall, Gregory Hines, and Bobby Short, addressed the vogue for old black popular songs. One failed retrospective, *Perfectly Frank*, served up the best of Frank Loesser, but poor handling and the effect of taking some of his fine material out of context led to a short run. Most noteworthy were two revues which, again, were not strictly speaking retrospectives, but which trafficked heavily in nostalgia. The more off-beat and successful of the two was *A Day in Hollywood/A Night in the Ukraine*. Perhaps qualifying the revue's claim to being a retrospective is unjust, for, like *Bubbling Brown Sugar*, an argument can be proffered that it, too, was a retrospective of a time and place, Hollywood in its halcyon years. Act

One—that day in Hollywood—sang song after song from treasured musical films (with some new Jerry Herman material injected for good measure). Act Two, though it professed to move to the Ukraine, kept its feet firmly in Hollywood, spoofing a Russian film as only the Marx Brothers could have. Groucho, Harpo, and Chico were deftly and daffily impersonated by three talented youngsters from the small-cast (eight), chorusless entertainment. Remarkably, this sometimes zany, sometimes warmhearted salute to American institutions was an importation from London.

Tintypes had great charm but, unfortunately, not much staying power when it moved from off-Broadway. An even more intimate production than *Day/Night*, with only six in the cast, it made a beguiling, glowing evening out of a grabbag of songs from the Gay Nineties to World War I (with one brief leap back to 1876 for "I'll Take You Home Again, Kathleen"). At its best the show captured the unashamed romanticism, the patriot fervor, and zesty gaiety of the period's more cherishable moments.

The curtain went up on 1981 to disclose an unusual offering. *Shakespeare's Cabaret* reached too far back to be considered nostalgia and, like 1963's *The Golden Age*, was too far from mainstream theatre to appeal to a large number of playgoers. That this revue of songs from Shakespeare's plays tallied 54 performances at the tiny Bijou was remarkable. But by any except academic standards the revue was a freak. Equally off the beaten track (and offered at the same house) was *Aaah Oui Genty!*, a French marionette revue. The year also welcomed briefly revivals of *Jacques Brel . . .* , and *This Was Burlesque*. An English comic, Dave Allen, failed to please with his one-man show, while *Broadway Follies*, a vaudeville featuring mostly foreign performers, and *The Moony Shapiro Songbook*, an English revue with a thin story line, shared the unwanted distinction of closing after the first performance. Aside from *This Was Burlesque*, all these revues had an imported tinge to them.

Not so the year's two big hits. Both were 100 percent American, and black American at that. *Sophisticated Ladies* was a tribute to the music of Duke Ellington. The title of *Lena Horne: The Lady and Her*

Music speaks for itself. Both, obviously, were retrospectives (though the latter must also be classified as basically a one-woman show). But Miss Horne's show brings up a very touchy matter. No solo show in years received the critical kudos lavished on Miss Horne, an entertainer who always delighted the eye and the ear in films. And the public responded with record-breaking attendance. Along with her excellent notices, her show's drawing power may stem in large measure from her celebrity as a film star. Look, for example, at a similar outpouring when Judy Garland and other film favorites appeared at the Palace and elsewhere years back. Even the huge success of Mickey Rooney and Ann Miller in *Sugar Babies* set side by side with the failure of the road company with Broadway's Carol Channing and Robert Morse suggests a similar conclusion. Of course, there is no reason why film stars should not be welcomed, but their background and possibly their training exacerbate and underline a horror that has become a dreaded Broadway musical commonplace in recent years—microphoning and amplification. In Miss Horne's case this problem was dramatically underscored, for her one-woman show was offered to New Yorkers at a tiny theatre that was built not for musicals but for smaller comedies and dramas (although it has since housed some fine intimate revues). Yet she clung to a microphone and was amplified. Was she unable to reach the last row or unwilling to make the effort? Of course, even the most supposedly realistic theatre is artificial, an especially pertinent truism when musicals are involved. After all, we do not normally sing our feelings to our friends and associates or break into a dance to tell a story. These departures are fundamentally artistic conventions. Scenery and costumes in musicals are usually stylized, colored, and coordinated beyond anything in the world outside. Again departures from reality, albeit this time largely decorative. But all of this applies to a very large extent to film and television musicals as well. What sets theatre apart is that it is, or should be, totally live. We come to the theatre to see flesh and blood actors talking, seemingly naturally, to each other, but in fact to us. Once technology intrudes with miking and amplification, theatre is no longer genuinely live theatre. One might as well listen at home to an original cast recording (much more comfortable and cheaper) or wait for a film or television version. Carried to a horrifying, logical extreme "live" theatre might just as well put the whole show on film and claim it is somehow live entertainment (at appropriate prices, no doubt). Indeed, several seasons back one star was accused of not really singing on stage, but simply mouthing a song in "sync" with a recording played over the amplifiers. And a touring musical recently had the same charge leveled at it.

On tour Miss Horne exemplified another disgraceful turn of affairs in contemporary theatre. Her show was so intimate that it could have been presented as easily in a minuscule cabaret as in a small legitimate house. But on the road her show sought out the hugest houses—often converted film palaces and similar mammoth auditoriums. Thus, having destroyed the immediacy of sound by microphoning she now deprived many admirers of that visual intimacy afforded by smaller playhouses. She was far from alone in this. Musical after musical followed the same shameful path, so she alone should not be accused. The greed of producers, writers, theatre owners, and other performers runs rampant. They all seem to have adopted a playgoing-public-be-damned attitude.

On the greater theatrical stage, the stage as a whole, these problems—the faddism in ignoring or deprecating the riches of our past theatre, miking and amplification, the playing in absurdly inappropriate auditoriums—these problems reflect the malaise that has bedeviled the modern American musical revue. As we have said, the difficulties are basic and twofold: the loss of the old sense of balance and of the old sense of proper purpose. From the start Broadway understood the proper purpose of the revue—to provide an evening of essentially escapist entertainment. In later years some of the best revues occasionally injected biting, touching social comment, but one or two such songs or skits tucked away in an otherwise carefree evening not only did not hurt the show but, by dramatically, if briefly, offering a message, all the more effectively underscored the message. In the 1930s the grotesque left-wing slanting of a revue such as *Parade* dissuaded both most critics and playgoers, and even the comparatively less vitriolic *Pins and Needles* achieved its long run by playing in a minuscule theatre and luring many non-traditional playgoers, who often made repeat visits because the producers cleverly kept inserting new updated material. For all its fame and its long run, *Pins and Needles* cannot be considered a truly mainstream, big-time Broadway revue. It was a child of its era. The occasional revue of recent years that trafficked heavily in social protest or comment rarely ran long, and those that did simply suggested that Broadway could accept more variegated fare than it once would. But the real successes of recent years have largely been revues that aimed first and foremost to entertain. Yet they managed to entertain all the while something was drastically out of kilter.

Because the very earliest American revues were perceived as offering acceptable entertainment, the genre was given time to develop and to find the best formula for complete success. Finding that formula took well over a decade and did not come about until Florenz Ziegfeld hit upon the answer. The *Follies* were almost certainly the first American revues to offer an unbeatable combination of wonderful casts, fine comedy, good dancing, beautiful scenery and costumes, and enduring songs. The largesse behind Ziegfeld's opulence may be unthinkable today, his lavish beauty sadly a thing of the past unless theatrical economics change, but we have discovered that eye-filling stage pictures need not be accomplished with the heavy brush of the Ziegfeldian era. Less may really not be more, but it can be indeed attractive. Curiously it was the enduring song that was the last piece of the puzzle to fall into place. To a large degree that was because there were precious few great composers, composers whose melodies live on, around when the genre was in its infancy. The still popular songs that Ziegfeld introduced in his early *Follies* were not always the work of composers identified primarily with Broadway but came rather from Tin Pan Alley. Think of "Shine On, Harvest Moon," "By the Light of the Silvery Moon," and "Row, Row, Row." And the later loss of enduring songs was to mark the beginning of the decline of the traditional revue.

None of the handful of humdrum offerings presented in 1982 or 1983 offered the slightest hope of a renaissance. And in 1984 Broadway saw nothing at all that could pass for a revue. So it well may be that like the long gone masque or the sensational melodrama or even the more recently disappeared high comedy the revue belongs simply to history. Only time will tell.

Meanwhile, let's be thankful for what the great revues have left behind. Pick your own favorite revue songs. The list is far too imposing and long even to begin to make suggestions here. Read the most literate and witty of the published skits—such as "If Men Played Cards As Women Do." Recall, if you were lucky enough to have seen them, the great clowns at their uproarious best. Browse through books which have pictured some of the scenic glories. And while basking in that thankful glow, is it wrong, also, to be a wee bit hopeful?

Appendix

This appendix offers a selective list of major Broadway revues. Solo shows have not been included.

Although most early revues listed "book" in their credits and did in fact have slight stories, here we have used the term "sketches" throughout. In some cases songs and sketches by authors not listed were also included.

The Passing Show. Music by Ludwig Englander; lyrics and sketches by Sydney Rosenfeld. Casino Theatre. May 12, 1894. Jefferson De Angelis, John Henshaw, Adele Ritchie, Madge Lessing, Queenie Vassar. Principal songs: "Old Before His Time," "Sex Against Sex." 110 performances.

In Gay New York. Music by Gustave Kerker; lyrics and sketches by Hugh Morton. Casino Theatre. May 25, 1896. Virginia Earle, Madge Lessing, Walter Jones, David Warfield, Richard Carle, Lee Harrison. Principal songs: "Girlie Girl," "It's Forty Miles from Schenectady to Troy," "Jusqu'la," "Molly." 120 performances.

About Town. Music by Melville Ellis and Raymond Hubbell; lyrics and sketches by Joseph Herbert. Herald Square Theatre. August 30, 1906. Lew Fields, Lawrence Grossmith, Jack Norworth, Vernon Castle, Louise Dresser, Edna Wallace Hopper. Principal songs: "The Girl in the Baby-Blue Tights," "I'm Sorry." 138 performances.

Follies of 1907. Music and lyrics by various hands; sketches by Harry B. Smith. Jardin de Paris (New York Theatre Roof). July 8, 1907. Harry Watson, Jr., David Lewis, Grace LaRue, Emma Carus, Mlle. Dazie, Annabelle Whitford. Principal songs: "Be Good! (If You Can't Be Good, Be Careful)," "Budweiser's a Friend of Mine," "I Think I Oughtn't Auto Anymore." 70 performances.

La Belle Paree. Music by Jerome Kern and Frank Tours; lyrics by Edward Madden; sketches by Edgar Smith. Winter Garden Theatre. March 20, 1911. Al Jolson, Lee Harrison, Barney Bernard, Stella Mayhew, Mitzi Hajos, Mlle. Dazie, Kitty Gordon. Principal songs: "I'm the Human Brush," "Look Me Over Dearie," "Paris Is a Paridise for Coons." 104 performances.

Hello, Broadway!. Music, lyrics, and sketches by George M. Cohan. Astor Theatre. December 25, 1914. George M. Cohan, William Collier, Louise Dresser, Rozsika Dolly, Peggy Wood, Florence Moore. Principal songs: "Broadway Tipperary," "Down by the Erie Canal," "Hello, Broadway!," "Those Irving Berlin Melodies." 123 performances.

The Passing Show of 1915. Music by various hands; lyrics and sketches by Harold Atteridge. Winter Garden Theatre. May 29, 1915. Marilyn Miller, John Charles Thomas, Willie and Eugene Howard. Principal songs: "America First," "First Love Is the Best Love of All," "Gamble on Me," "Panama-Pacific Drag." 145 performances.

Ziegfeld Follies of 1919. Music by Irving Berlin and others; lyrics by Berlin and others; sketches by various hands. New Amsterdam Theatre. June 16, 1919. Eddie Cantor, Eddie Dowling, Ray Dooley, Marilyn Miller, John Steel, Van and Schenck, Bert Williams. Principal songs: "Mandy," "My Baby's Arms," "A Pretty Girl Is Like a Melody," "Tulip Time," "You Cannot Make Your Shimmy Shake on Tea," "You'd Be Surprised." 171 performances.

The Greenwich Village Follies. Music by A. Baldwin Sloane; lyrics by Arthur Swanstrom and John Murray Anderson; sketches by Anderson and Philip Bartholomae. Greenwich Village Theatre. July 15, 1919. Bessie McCoy Davis, James Watts, Ted Lewis and His Orchestra. Principal songs: "I Want a Daddy Who Will Rock Me to Sleep," "Red as the Rose," "When My Baby Smiles at Me." 232 performances.

Music Box Revue. Music and lyrics by Irving Berlin; sketches by various hands. Music Box Theatre. September 22, 1921. William Collier, Sam Bernard, Wilda Bennett, Florence Moore, Joseph Santley, Ivy Sawyer. Principal songs: "Everybody Step," "In a Cozy Kitchenette Apartment," "Say It with Music," "They Call It Dancing." 440 performances.

Chauve-Souris. A revue by and with Russian post-revolution émigrés, headed by Nikita Balieff. 49th Street Theatre. February 4, 1922. Principal song: "Parade of the Wooden Soldiers." 520 performances.

Earl Carroll's Vanities of 1923. Music and lyrics mainly by Carroll; sketches mainly by William Collier. Earl Carroll Theatre. July 5, 1923. Joe Cook,

Bernard Granville, Peggy Hopkins Joyce. Principal songs: "My Cretonne Girl," "Pretty Peggy." 204 performances.

Charlot's Revue. Music, lyrics and sketches by various hands. Times Square Theatre. January 9, 1924. Beatrice Lillie, Gertrude Lawrence, Jack Buchanan. Principal songs: "Limehouse Blues," "March with Me," "Parisian Pierrot." 285 performances.

The Garrick Gaieties. Music by Richard Rodgers; lyrics by Lorenz Hart; sketches by various hands. Garrick Theatre. June 8, 1925. Sterling Holloway, Romney Brent, Philip Loeb, Libby Holman, June Cochrane, Edith Meiser, Rose Rolando, Stanford Meisner, Lee Strasberg. Principal songs: "Manhattan," "Sentimental Me." 211 performances.

George White's Scandals of 1926. Music by Ray Henderson; lyrics by B. G. DeSylva and Lew Brown; sketches by George White and William K. Wells. Apollo Theatre. June 14, 1926. Ann Pennington, Tom Patricola, Willie and Eugene Howard, Harry Richman, Frances Williams. Principal songs: "The Birth of the Blues," "Black Bottom," "The Girl Is You and the Boy Is Me," "Lucky Day." 424 performances.

Blackbirds of 1928. Music by Jimmy McHugh; lyrics by Dorothy Fields; few small sketches uncredited but probably by Miss Fields. Liberty Theatre. May 9, 1928. Adelaide Hall, Bill Robinson, Aida Ward, Tim Moore, Hall Johnson Choir. Principal songs: "Diga Diga Do," "Doin' the New Low Down," "I Can't Give You Anything But Love," "I Must Have That Man." 518 performances.

The Little Show. Music by Arthur Schwartz and others; lyrics by Howard Dietz and others; sketches by Dietz, George S. Kaufman, and Newman Levy. Music Box Theatre. April 30, 1929. Clifton Webb, Fred Allen, Libby Holman, Romney Brent, Bettina Hall. Principal songs: "Can't We Be Friends?," "I Guess I'll Have To Change My Plan," "Moanin' Low." 331 performances.

Three's a Crowd. Music by Arthur Schwartz and others; lyrics by Howard Dietz and others; sketches by Dietz and others. Selwyn Theatre. October 15, 1930. Clifton Webb, Fred Allen, Libby Holman. Principal songs: "Body and Soul," "Something To Remember You By." 272 performances.

The Band Wagon. Music by Arthur Schwartz; lyrics by Howard Dietz; sketches by Dietz and George S. Kaufman. New Amsterdam Theatre. June 3, 1931. Fred and Adele Astaire, Frank Morgan, Helen Broderick, Tilly Losch. Principal songs: "Dancing in the Dark," "High and Low," "I Love Louisa," "New Sun in the Sky," "Where Can He Be?" 260 performances.

As Thousands Cheer. Music and lyrics by Irving Berlin; sketches by Moss Hart. Music Box Theatre. September 30, 1933. Marilyn Miller, Ethel Waters, Helen Broderick, Clifton Webb, José Limon. Principal songs: "Easter Parade," "Harlem on My Mind," "Heat Wave," "Not for All the Rice in China," "Supper Time." 400 performances.

Life Begins at 8:40. Music by Harold Arlen; lyrics by Ira Gershwin and E. Y. Harburg; sketches by David Freedman and others. Winter Garden Theatre. August 27, 1934. Bert Lahr, Ray Bolger, Luella Gear, Frances Williams. Principal songs: "I Couldn't Hold My Man," "You're a Builder-Upper." 237 performances.

At Home Abroad. Music by Arthur Schwartz; lyrics by Howard Dietz; sketches by Dietz and others. Winter Garden Theatre. September 19, 1935. Beatrice Lillie, Ethel Waters, Eleanor Powell, Reginald Gardiner. Principal songs: "Farewell My Lovely," "Get Yourself a Geisha," "Got a Bran' New Suit," "Hottentot Potentate," "Thief in the Night." 198 performances.

The Show Is On. Music, lyrics, and sketches by various hands. Winter Garden Theatre. December 25, 1936. Beatrice Lillie, Bert Lahr, Reginald Gardiner. Principal songs: "By Strauss," "Little Old Lady," "Song of the Woodman." 237 performances.

Pins and Needles. Music and lyrics by Harold Rome; sketches by various hands. Labor Stage. November 27, 1937. Cast consisted of members of ILGWU. Principal songs: "Sing Me a Song with Social Significance," "Sunday in the Park." 1,108 performances.

Hellzapoppin. Music by Sammy Fain; lyrics by Charles Tobias; sketches by Ole Olsen and Chic Johnson. 46th Street Theatre. September 22, 1938. Olsen and Johnson. No major songs. 1,404 performances.

This Is the Army. Music and lyrics by Irving Berlin; virtually no sketches. Broadway Theatre. July 4, 1942. All soldier cast. Principal new songs: "I Left My Heart at the Stage Door Canteen," "I'm Getting Tired So I Can Sleep," "This Is the Army, Mr. Jones." ("Mandy" and "Oh, How I Hate To Get Up in the Morning" revived from World War I all-soldier show, *Yip, Yip, Yaphank.*) 113 performances.

Call Me Mister. Music and lyrics by Harold Rome; sketche by Arnold Auerbach and Arnold Horwitt. National Theatre. April 18, 1946. Jules Munshin, Betty Garrett. Principal songs: "The Face on the Dime," "South America, Take It Away." 734 performances.

Angel in the Wings. Music and lyrics by Bob Hillard and Carl Sigman; sketches by Ted Luce, Hank Ladd, Paul and Grace Hartman. Coronet Theatre. December 11, 1947. Paul and Grace Hartman, Hank Ladd, Elaine Stritch. Principal songs: "The Big Brass Band from Brazil," "Civilization," "Thousand Islands Song." 308 performances.

Make Mine Manhattan. Music by Richard Lewine; lyrics and sketches by Arnold Horwitt. Broadhurst Theatre. January 15, 1948. Sid Caesar, David Burns, Joshua Shelley, Kyle MacDonnell. Principal songs: "Saturday Night in Central Park," "Subway Song," "Traftz." 429 performances.

Inside U.S.A.. Music by Arthur Schwartz; lyrics by Howard Dietz; sketches by Arnold Auerbach, Moss Hart, and Arnold Horwitt. Century Theatre. April 30, 1948. Beatrice Lillie, Jack Haley, Valerie Bettis, Herb Shriner, John Tyers. Principal songs: "First Prize at the Fair," "Haunted Heart," "Rhode Island Is Famous for You." 399 performances.

Lend an Ear. Music, lyrics, and sketches by Charles Gaynor. National Theatre. December 16, 1948. Carol Channing, Yvonne Adair, William Eythe, George Hall, Gene Nelson. Principal song: "Who Hit Me?" 460 performances.

Two on the Aisle. Music by Jule Styne; lyrics and sketches mostly by Betty Comden and Adolph Green. Mark Hellinger Theatre. July 19, 1951. Bert Lahr, Dolores Gray, Elliot Reid. Principal songs: "Give a Little, Get a Little Love," "If You Hadn't, But You Did." 281 performances.

New Faces of 1952. Music, lyrics, and sketches by various hands. Royale Theatre. May 16, 1952. Ronny Graham, Eartha Kitt, Robert Clary, Alice Ghostley, Carol Lawrence, Paul Lynde. Principal songs: "Boston Beguine," "Monotonous," "Lizzie Borden," "Love Is a Simple Thing." 365 performances.

John Murray Anderson's Almanac. Music, lyrics and sketches by various hands. Imperial Theatre. December 10, 1953. Hermione Gingold, Billy DeWolfe, Harry Belafonte, Polly Bergen, Orson Bean. Principal song: "Hold 'Em, Joe." 229 performances.

Shoestring Revue. Music, lyrics and sketches by various hands. President Theatre. February 28, 1955. Dorothy Greener, Arte Johnson, Beatrice Arthur, Dody Goodman, Chita Rivera. No memorable songs. 88 performances.

La Plume de Ma Tante. Music by Gerard Calvi; sketches by Robert Dhery. Royale Theatre. November 11, 1958. Robert Dhery, Colette Brosset, Pierre Olaf. No memorable songs. 835 performances.

Beyond the Fringe. Sketches written by the performers. John Golden Theatre. October 27, 1962. Alan Bennett, Peter Cook, Dudley Moore, Jonathan Miller. No songs. 667 performances.

The Decline and Fall of the Entire World as Seen Through the Eyes of Cole Porter Revisited. Music and lyrics by Cole Porter, with continuity by Bud McCreery. Square East Theatre. March 30, 1965. This show used a collection of old Porter songs, mostly lesser known works. 273 performances.

Bubbling Brown Sugar. Music by various hands, with continuity by Loften Mitchell. ANTA Theatre. March 2, 1976. Avon Long, Josephine Premice. New songs intermingled with older songs by black writers. 766 performances.

Side by Side by Sondheim. Music largely by Stephen Sondheim; lyrics by Sondheim. Music Box Theatre. April 18, 1977. David Kernan, Millicent Martin, Julie N. McKenzie, Ned Sherrin. A retrospective of Sondheim work. 384 performances.

Dancin'. Music from various sources, old and new. Broadhurst Theatre. March 27, 1978. Ann Reinking. An evening of dances, all choreographed by Bob Fosse. 1,774 performances.

Ain't Misbehavin'. Music mainly by Fats Waller; lyrics by various hands. Longacre Theatre. May 9, 1978. Nell Carter, Ken Page. A retrospective of Waller favorites. 1,604 performances.

Eubie! Music by Eubie Blake; lyrics by various hands. Ambassador Theatre. September 20, 1978. Gregory and Maurice Hines, Lonnie McNeil. A retrospective of Blake works. 439 performances.

Sugar Babies. Music and lyrics by various hands; sketches by Ralph G. Allen. Mark Hellinger Theatre. October 8, 1979. Mickey Rooney, Ann Miller. 1,208 performances.

Sophisticated Ladies. Music by Duke Ellington; lyrics by various hands. Lunt-Fontanne Theatre. March 1, 1981. Hinton Battle, Gregory Hines, Judith Jamison, Mercedes Ellington. An Ellington retrospective. 767 performances.

Index

Hoctor, Harriet, 102
Hoffman, "Think a Drink," 114
"Hold 'Em, Joe," 140
"Hold Me in Your Loving Arms," 43
Holloway, Stanley, 147
Holman, Libby, 89, 90, 141
"Hoops," 92
Hooray for What!, 106
Holtz, Lou, 77
Hope, Bob, 102, 103, 114
Hopkins, Linda, 154
Hopkins, Miriam, 82
Hopkinson, Francis, 6
Hopper, Edna Wallace, 27
Hopper DeWolf, 74
Hornblow, Arthur, 81
Horne, Lena, 163–64
Horwitt, Arnold, 109
"Hottentot Potentate," 100
"How High the Moon," 114
Howard, Eugene, and/or Willie, 71, 74, 77, 78, 96, 115, 122
"How'd You Like To Take Me Home . . . ," 32
Howland, Jobyna, 71
Hubbell, Raymond, 27
Hurok, Sol, 126

"I Can't Get Started," 103
"I Can't Give You Anything But Love," 87
"I Couldn't Hold My Man," 98
"I Gotta Right To Sing the Blues," 85
"I Guess I'll Have To Change My Plan," 89
"I Left My Heart at the Stage Door Canteen," 120
"I Love Louisa," 92, 93
"I Love My Love in the Springtime," 18
"I Think I Oughtn't Auto Anymore," 32
"I Want To Be a Drummer Boy," 34
"I Was a Florodora Baby," 48
"If Men Played Cards as Women Do," 83, 92, 166
"If This Is Glamour," 134
"If You Hadn't, But You Did," 136
"I'll Be True to You," 132
"I'll Build a Stairway . . . ," 76
"I'll Take You Home Again . . . ," 162
"I'm Forever Blowing Bubbles," 74
"I'm Getting Tired . . . ," 120
"I'm an Indian," 48

"I'm in Love Again," 59
"In Bed with the Reader's Digest," 141
In Circles, 151
In Gay New York, 22–23, 25
In Gayest Manhattan, 25
"In Our Teeny Little Weeny Nest," 131
Inside U.S.A., 120, 130
International Ladies' Garment Workers Union, 107
Ipi-Tombi, 157
Irving, George S., 134
"Island in the West Indies," 102
"Isle D'Amour," 84
It Happens on Ice, 116
"It Will Be All Right," 135
"It's Forty Miles . . . ," 23
"I've Been to a Marvelous Party," 113
Ives, Burl, 121, 127

Jackson, Arthur, 76
Jacques Brel Is Alive . . ., 151, 162
James, Paul, 89
Janis, Elsie, 59, 97
Jessel, George, 122
John Murray Anderson's Almanac, 139–40
Johnson, Albert, 91, 92, 95, 97, 98
Johnson, Arte, 142
Johnson, Chic, *see* Olsen and Johnson
Johnson, Van, 103
Johnstone, Justine, 36
"Join Us in a [Little] Cup . . . ," 131, 147
Jolson, Al, 54
Jones, T. C., 142, 143
Jones, Walter, 22
"Jusqu' la," 23

Kahn, Otto, 60
Kander and Ebb, 160
Kaufman, George S., 62, 83, 88, 91, 92, 112, 126
Kaye, Danny, 116
Keep 'Em Laughing, 122
Keep Off the Grass, 116
Kelly, Gene, 113
Kelly, Patsy, 85, 93
Kerker, Gustave, 22, 26, 27
Kern, Jerome, 26, 57
Kerr, Walter and Jean, 135
Kert, Larry, 154
Kill That Fly!, 64